SAM SMITH

SAM SMITH
THE BIOGRAPHY

JOE ALLAN

JOHN BLAKE

Published by John Blake Publishing Ltd,
3 Bramber Court, 2 Bramber Road,
London W14 9PB, England

www.johnblakebooks.com

www.facebook.com/johnblakebooks ⨍
twitter.com/jblakebooks ⨏

This edition published in 2015

ISBN: 978 1 78418 772 9

British Library Cataloguing-in-Publication Data:

A catalogue record for this book is available from the British Library.

Design by www.envydesign.co.uk

Printed in Great Britain by CPI Group (UK) Ltd

1 3 5 7 9 10 8 6 4 2

The right of Joe Al... the author of this work has been asserted by him in accordance with the Copyright, Designs and Patents Act 1988.

Papers used by John ... Publishing are natural, recyclable products made from wood grown in su... ... conform to the environmental regulations of the country of origin.

Every attempt ... made to ... ...-holders, but some we... ... ... We would be grateful if the appropriate people would contact us.

To Doug. From a brother who
was once a bother.

CONTENTS

TAKE ME FOR WHAT I AM

'There's something very pure and direct about the way Sam lives his life, and he's very transparent in his portrayal of his image.'
Taylor Swift on why she quickly became one of Sam Smith's number one fans – *Rolling Stone*, January 2015

On 8 February 2015, as 'Stay With Me' was announced as the winner of the prestigious 'Record of the Year' award at the 57th Grammy Awards in Los Angeles, Sam Smith returned to the stage of the Staples Center, Los Angeles, to accept his fourth trophy of the night.

While the speech he made once he'd reached the podium, thanking the man who had broken his heart and inspired him to create most of the songs featured on his debut album, *In the Lonely Hour*, was the focus of much of the media and press coverage which followed, Sam's multiple trips to the stage earlier in the evening, to pick up his other awards, were equally noteworthy and demonstrated just how far he'd come in a relatively short period of time.

Receiving his 'Best New Artist' award from presenter Taylor Swift, who'd already declared he was 'her absolute new favourite' when she invited him to join her onstage for a duet of his 'Money On My Mind' track at her London show the previous month, Sam appeared both suitably shocked and understandably elated to be receiving any form of recognition from his peers.

And as if enjoying BFF status with the biggest-selling pop artist in the world wasn't enough, over the course of that one night his position within the pecking order of the gathered music business glitterati appeared to be shifting, rising sharply in a matter of hours. On the few steps required to get him from his designated seat in the audience – fortuitously situated in close proximity to the stage – Sam air-kissed and hugged a veritable 'Who's-Who' of the music industry's biggest stars, including Lady Gaga, Rihanna and Katy Perry, as well as the aforementioned Taylor Swift.

It was truly a dream come true for the twenty-two-year-old who, only a year or so earlier, had been struggling to get a foothold on even the lowest rung of the industry ladder, working full-time in a London bar and dreaming of becoming a world-famous singer. While easy comparisons could be made with Adele, the UK's other recent multiple Grammy Award winning success story, Sam's journey to acceptance and worldwide acclaim was decidedly different.

Unlike Adele, and so many of the UK's artists who have enjoyed commercial success and critical acclaim, both internationally and at home in recent years (Amy Winehouse, Leona Lewis, Jessie J and Katie Melua, among many more), Sam Smith wasn't groomed for success at the esteemed BRIT School. He hadn't attended any of the UK's many music or drama colleges and he certainly didn't possess any formal qualifications that might suggest he was destined for success as a musician, specifically, or anywhere within the music business in general. In fact, he didn't even know how to play a musical instrument. But he had a voice. And while his rise may seem like a classic overnight success story, he had actually been developing his extraordinary vocal style for most of his life.

After discovering an early aptitude for mimicry, copying and often matching the power and range of some of pop music's greatest vocalists, Sam had been encouraged to further develop his natural skills and eventually found his own voice. Far from being an instant sensation, he had been trying to make it as a professional singer for close to a decade before he made his UK chart debut as a featured vocalist on 'Latch', the breakthrough hit for Surrey-born dance duo, Disclosure, in late 2012.

Sam's early promise had been spotted by his parents, Fred and Kate, who decided to nurture their son's talent (and obvious interest in all things dramatic) by encouraging him to take singing lessons and to explore the world of musical theatre. After several years picking up invaluable tips and experiences, first as a backing singer for his singing tutor, and later performing whenever and wherever anyone was willing to listen, he began to attract attention from numerous artist managers who believed that he was destined for big things.

A decade of unfulfilled dreams and the inevitable disappointment that followed saw Sam work his way through a handful of management teams before he had even turned eighteen years old. His confidence shattered, Sam was fairly jaded about the idea of continuing to chase his dream, and wary of the music industry as a whole.

At over six foot tall and having struggled with his weight as a child and well into his teens, Sam knew he would never be a traditional, 'pretty-boy' pop star. Physically, he was a million miles away from the likes of Olly Murs or the boys from One Direction and his ambitions as a singer were similarly far removed from the 'quick fix', overnight fame offered by producer and mentor Simon Cowell and reality TV shows such as *The X Factor, Britain's Got Talent* or *The Voice.*

As confidence in his own abilities returned, buoyed by his newly forged relationships with several like-minded and similarly ambitious underground artists, contemporary songwriters and producers, as well as a new team of managers, Sam began to trust his own instincts about the type of artist he wanted to become. He wished to emulate the careers of his musical idols, the likes of Whitney Houston, Chaka Khan, Dinah Washington and most of all, Beyoncé. Sam wanted longevity as an artist. Determined his voice would be the thing people remembered, not how he looked or which designer outfits he was wearing, he wanted the people who bought his records to believe every word he sang, and understand that those words came directly from his heart and soul. He had first-hand experience of the type of pressure placed upon new artists to invent a separate 'media persona', in order to create an air of mystery about them and ultimately give a hyped sense of who they really were to the public.

Previously, he had been advised by former managers about his image and choice of song. Now, he was determined to give his fans the real deal. He had no interest in creating what he saw as a false public persona, vowing instead to remain open and candid about who he was, and what he chose to sing about. Years of training and countless hours of practice had led him to the realisation that honesty and truthfulness were the key ingredients to his performance as a singer. And now, by revealing himself emotionally and channelling his own vulnerability within the lyrics of his songs, he was much more likely to make the type of natural and meaningful connection he wanted to make with his audience.

Sam's debut album, *In the Lonely Hour* – a collection of self-penned songs, exposing some painfully raw nerves and divulging the type of secrets about life and love that even the most candid artists might shy away from – would become the only album of 2014 to sell more than a million copies on both sides of the Atlantic, and was to catapult him emphatically into the spotlight and onto the world stage with dizzying speed and to dramatic effect. Sam Smith is now reaping the rewards for years of hard work, dogged perseverance and almost unfaltering self-belief. The road from his debut solo release 'Nirvana' to *In the Lonely Hour* and beyond has been a long and turbulent one, but perhaps that selfie with Taylor Swift just about makes it all worthwhile.

CHAPTER ONE

GO YOUR OWN WAY

'It's never felt like a job, it's never even felt like an interest.
When people ask me, "Do you love singing?" I don't
know because it's like second nature.'
Sam Smith on why he became a singer – *Hunger TV*, June 2014

In early September 2014, less than three months after the US release of his debut album, *In the Lonely Hour*, Sam Smith was escorting a camera crew from America's CBS TV network around the quiet English village of Great Chishill in south Cambridgeshire. His album had made its chart debut at No.2 on the US Billboard Top 200, selling more than 166,000 copies in its first week of release, and became the fastest selling debut by a UK male artist in US chart history, instantly turning him into a household name in the process. It's hardly surprising, considering his recent rapid rise to international stardom, that his arrival in this normally peaceful and sleepy rural beauty spot was a little unexpected, caused something of a commotion and left a few of the locals bemused and mildly 'star-struck'. But this was where Sam had spent most of his childhood and it was while growing up in these undeniably idyllic surroundings he'd discovered an early passion and aptitude for singing.

Sam had returned to his home village in order to film a piece for the CBS Network show, *Sunday Morning*. As he revisited some of his old haunts, sharing his earliest memories and recalling some of the people and events which had exerted an early, guiding influence on him, host Anthony Mason asked him, 'What was the plan?' Without a second's hesitation Sam said, 'The plan was to move to London and become a famous singer.' For Sam Smith, at the tender age of twenty-two, it was pretty much 'mission accomplished'. But he would be the first to admit putting his apparently straightforward and unwavering plan into action was far from plain sailing. In order to live out his fantasy, complete with fairytale ending – to move to the big city, where all his dreams would come true – he would have to work harder than he could possible imagine and, along the way, there would be more than a few harsh realities to deal with.

When Samuel Fredrick Smith was born, on 19 May 1992, his parents, Frederick (Fred) Smith and Katherine (Kate) Cassidy, were living in a fairly modest two-bedroom house in the picturesque village of Linton, south Cambridgeshire. Sam was their first child and his birth signalled a fairly dramatic change of circumstances for the entire Smith household. Sam's mother, Kate, had started her working life as a clerk at Barclays Bank, but her ultimate goal saw her aiming a lot higher: eventually she would make her mark in the world of high finance.

For Kate is descended from a clan of extremely strong and

pioneering females, among which were some of the first women to break into the male-dominated world of financial trading. It would appear she had inherited much of their spirit and was similarly passionate and ambitious by nature. It was these traits that made her incredibly driven and focused, ensuring she excelled at everything she turned her attention to and easily over-achieved when it came to reaching her professional goals. Confident and perceptively intelligent, she had all the right characteristics to survive in the notoriously cutthroat world of finance and market trading. Her determination to succeed was more than matched by her enormous potential and soon she began to flourish.

Kate's progression sent her on a steady upward trajectory, eventually leading to her becoming one of the few women in the nineties working as a London City trader. Although she was working in an area of the business still regarded as a predominately male environment, there was no doubt she could hold her own. She was good at what she did and progressed quickly. Her apparent determination to make a better life for herself and her family never faltered and seems to have merely intensified as her career went from strength to strength. By the time Sam had celebrated his third birthday, and his little sister Lily Jane had come along a month earlier in April 1995, their mother was now the main breadwinner.

Sam's dad, Fred, who is reported to have previously provided for his family by working as a security guard and running a fruit and vegetable stall in Fulham, would ultimately give up all full-time work and effectively become a stay-at-home-dad, choosing to look after the day-to-day business of bringing up the kids and keeping the family home running smoothly. As their financial situation improved – with Kate's annual salary reportedly hitting £200,000 even before substantial bonuses eventually increased her estimated earnings to more than £500,000 per year – it became apparent the family had outgrown their current living arrangements and the decision was made to upgrade and buy a bigger house nearby.

Sam and the rest of his family moved a few miles south to the equally charming village of Great Chishill and there was no doubt about it, they were definitely moving up in the world. But with another baby on the way, it would seem the move was prompted as much by necessity as extravagance. By the time Sam's second sister, Mabel, had arrived, the family had moved into an eighteenth century, Grade II-listed, four-bedroom cottage with a large, quarter-acre garden, an altogether more spacious and unquestionably far grander kind of accommodation.

This would be where Sam grew up, in what he would later call 'The Pink House' due to its external paint job. It remained Sam's family home, shared with his parents and two sisters, until he turned eighteen, when he moved out and relocated to London. While many have suggested his background was moneyed and his upbringing might seem somewhat privileged, it's safe to say it wasn't always that way and any upturn in the Smith family's fortunes was simply a by-product of Kate's dogged determination and hard work.

Sam would later stress to the *Guardian*, 'I really do know more what it's like to be poor than I know what it's like to be rich,' admitting his family's change in circumstances came as a surprise to them all, as he stated, 'The climb to

GO YOUR OWN WAY

money was sudden,' before acknowledging, 'We were doing nicer things, building, travelling around the world.' Indeed, over the next few years, their new house expanded with the addition of a conservatory and the garden soon boasted a decent-sized swimming pool.

But in real terms the Smiths were merely taking advantage of having a little more money coming into the household and their new lifestyle could hardly be described as lavish or extravagant. Instead, the whole family was simply adapting to a new way of life and over the next few years, as they settled into their new home, it was obvious Sam, Lily and Mabel were simply being afforded the opportunity to grow up contented and well looked after. Rather than becoming spoilt or seeming entitled, instead they seemed nothing but grateful for the opportunities and new experiences which were now coming their way.

Perhaps viewed from the outside, Fred's decision to stay at home to look after the children might be viewed as a relatively unusual situation, but for Sam and his sisters it was simply the way it had always been. They were quick to accept their father being around the house all the time, presumably because they had nothing to compare it to, and this set-up was perfectly normal to them. Fred was well suited to the job, relishing his new role as house husband and it made Sam and his siblings' childhood relatively idyllic. Sam told *Pigeons and Planes*, 'I had the best childhood I could've asked for, it was incredible.'

By the time Sam was old enough to start school, it's safe to assume the Smith household was functioning like a well-oiled machine and, in order to get everyone exactly where they needed to be (and on time), the family's hectic morning routine needed to run like clockwork. With Kate up and out early, heading to London on her daily commute, it was Fred's responsibility to get Sam (and eventually his two sisters) to school. Sam was enrolled at St. Thomas More's, the local Catholic primary school in the nearby town of Saffron Walden, Essex, and Fred would make the twenty-mile round trip each morning to drop him off and then again in the afternoon to bring him home.

Rather than becoming a monotonous chore, it was on these regular car journeys where Sam must have first heard many of the legendary artists he would later count among his earliest inspirations and whom he credits with igniting his passion for singing. 'Music playing in the car,' Sam would tell *Bent* magazine, in an early interview when he was still only sixteen years old. 'I always say that the tape player in the car was the reason I sing today.' It was here, on the drive to and from school, where he first heard many of the singers and songs he would later cite as having the most profound and lasting impact on him, with many of the artists he was introduced to at this early stage – including such legendary artists as Ella Fitzgerald, Aretha Franklin and Dinah Washington – eventually becoming a major influence in the development of his own personal tastes and musical preferences.

While Sam was too young to fully appreciate what he was listening to – he admits his first specific memories of the actual singers and songs he was hearing came a little later – he was undoubtedly already absorbing the basic elements of the music his father was passionate about. Discussing some of his earliest memories, Sam revealed, 'I guess you could say my family listen to black music mostly and I would like to think that's where I got my voice from,' before joking, 'On the inside, I'm this warbling soul singer from the 60s.' Early exposure to some of the all-time greatest vocalists served as an unconventional and eclectic musical education, delivering some valuable lessons in voice control and powerful vocal delivery.

This was something, it's safe to assume, most of his classmates of the late nineties were not getting from their favourite bands, with the likes of Steps, S Club 7, 911 and Boyzone riding high in the UK charts at the time. And so it was, sitting in the back seat of his parents' car, the only place his entire family listened collectively and shared the music they loved, that Sam's musical journey begins. It was in this relaxed and non-judgemental environment where he recalls actually singing out loud for the first time. With no one censoring or criticising, it was here that he started to make the association between singing and feeling happy. Here he was truly himself, able to feel totally free and fully express himself. Obviously, at this point there was no pressure or assumption being made in terms of his pursuing his singing beyond the point of merely being a hobby. Sam's parents accepted it was simply an enjoyable activity to pass the time on boring car journeys, but it was obvious to everyone around him that Sam was having fun and a seed had been sown, it would seem.

As time passed, and Sam and his sisters were getting a little older, the whole Smith family started to do a lot more travelling. They enjoyed several foreign holidays together as a family unit and Sam recalls seeing quite a lot of the world at a relatively young age. 'My mom and dad took me and my sisters everywhere as a kid,' he told *The Line of Best Fit*. 'I love seeing different places and eating different foods and experiencing different cultures.' Thus he recalls visiting Abu Dhabi to stay with friends of his mother, travelling holidays in Italy and Spain, as well as frequent trips to the United States. Of course this invariably involved lots of driving and long car journeys, giving him extra time to practise singing and even more of a stage on which to perform. It was during this period, around the time he turned eight years old, when Sam first heard the singer who would probably have the greatest impact on his own vocal style and has remained an obvious influence throughout his career to date. 'My first musical memory,' he recalled in an interview with *The Line of Best Fit*, 'was my mum playing Whitney Houston's *My Love Is Your Love* album in the car.'

Whitney Houston enjoyed a meteoric rise to fame in the mid-1980s when her song, 'Saving All My Love for You', hit No.1 on both sides of the Atlantic. In the US, she became the first female artist to score three No.1 hits from a debut album as her next two singles, 'How Will I Know' and 'The Greatest Love of All', also topped the Billboard Hot 100 chart and propelled her self-titled debut album to estimated total worldwide sales of over twenty-five million copies. In a way, it was hardly surprising that Whitney succeeded; she was part of a long-established musical dynasty which included her mother, gospel singer Cissy Houston, and her cousin, singer Dionne Warwick, as well as counting the likes of Aretha Franklin and Darlene Love among her 'honorary' extended family, But no one could have predicted just how all-consuming and ultimately self-destructive her celebrity would become.

During the 1990s Whitney had successfully diversified, establishing herself as a bankable lead actress with the massive box-office hit of 1992, *The Bodyguard*, but started to hit the headlines for all the wrong reasons, due to her volatile marriage to fellow pop singer Bobby Brown and escalating rumours regarding her erratic behaviour and suspected problems with drug abuse. Amid all the controversy, Houston would experience something of a renaissance with her 1998 album, *My Love Is Your Love*.

On its release in November of that year, *My Love Is Your Love* was Houston's first non-soundtrack studio album in almost a decade and by this stage in her career many in the music industry (and indeed among the record-buying public) had already written her off as old-fashioned and 'out of touch'. She had been associated with MOR ballads and slickly-produced pop-dance tracks, but the new album found her shrewdly collaborating with contemporary, credible artists, including Wyclef Jean, Missy Elliott, Lauren Hill, Faith Evans, Babyface and Rodney Jerkins. With its more modern-sounding production, *My Love Is Your Love* successfully repositioned Houston as a much edgier, cooler and more relevant urban artist. As well as being a major commercial success around the world, it provided her with some of the best reviews of her career. The broadening of her musical palette gave her increased exposure in the largely untapped urban market, helping her to reach a new, predominately younger audience, while the high quality of the material gathered for the album ensured she also reconnected with many of her lapsed, older fans.

Songs such as 'It's Not Right, But It's Okay', and especially the album's title track, were lyrically raw and uncharacteristically candid, hinting at some of Houston's own personal issues. As *Rolling Stone* stated in their album review, 'The former ingénue has some grown-up scars now, singing the marital blues with a bite in her voice that she's never come close to before.' Undoubtedly it was this relatable quality, a newly acquired vulnerability and openness, which helped Houston stage an unexpectedly more assured and successful comeback than anyone could have initially expected.

Mixing old-school soul, reggae, hip-hop and soaring R&B ballads, it's hardly surprising the album was a big hit in the Smith household, considering Sam's parents' long-established preference for soul music and black artists. But the album seemed to incite a particularly strong reaction in Sam, who later told *Vibe*, 'I was so obsessed,' inspiring him to listen to Houston's previous albums and investigate similar artists. Crucially, it was an influence that would clearly be heard on the more confessional and deeply personal lyrics of some of Sam's own material in the future.

Although Sam has revealed he rarely listened to any male vocalists at this time, he admitted to *Bent*, 'I adore Stevie Wonder and Prince,' and qualified it by saying he simply loved 'anyone with soul'. Thus, it was the big, soulful female voices that really made a stronger, lasting impression on the young Sam. Before too long, with encouragement from his parents, of course, he was discovering the delights of Aretha

Franklin, Dionne Warwick, Etta James, Dinah Washington and Chaka Khan. The latter was a particular favourite of Sam's mother, Kate. Sam, in an interview conducted by the legendary Chaka Khan herself in *V* magazine, recalled how Kate had predicted her son's future success by saying, 'It's all good. Sam's just got to get Chaka Khan to sing with him when I'm in my fifties.' Although this could be taken as a fairly light-hearted and off-the-cuff remark, considering Sam was merely singing casually for his own amusement at this stage, it indicates just how much faith his parents had in him from the very beginning. While it could be said neither Fred nor Kate themselves had any particularly interest or aptitude in terms of singing or performing music, their attitude towards their son's obvious fascination for the subject demonstrates an eagerness to accept his individuality and encourage him to develop his own passions.

Sam told *Hunger TV*, 'Despite not having any family member being musical, it was definitely in my blood,' adding, 'I don't remember not singing.' All this helps to paint a picture of a tight-knit and hugely supportive family, a stimulating atmosphere and the 'anything is possible' attitude which seems to have prevailed in the Smith household as Sam and his sisters grew up and were encouraged to develop their own interests and hobbies.

And so Sam was soon to embark on a very personal musical voyage of discovery. Subsequently, exposure to some of the most extraordinary and powerful female voices ever recorded had an inevitable effect on his own singing style, as well as the type of songs he wanted to sing. He told *The Line Of Best Fit*, 'I loved Chaka Khan's "Through The Fire",

Aretha's "Say A Little Prayer", Etta James' "All I Could Do Was Cry", that's one of my favourite songs of all time.'

Considering the charts were filled with boy bands and cheesy pop acts at the time, it's safe to say Sam was heading off on a very unique and distinctive musical path of his own. 'It was those powerful vocals from women that just always touched me from a young age,' he explained to *Hunger*. 'I don't know whether it was what they were saying or the certain tones of voices that got me,' before adding, 'It was something I wanted to do myself. Maybe it's the soul you hear in the voice – it just hits you.'

Whatever it was, Sam spent virtually every waking hour singing along with those enormous, soulful voices. He told *Interview* magazine, 'Every night after school I used to download backing tracks of songs I loved and perform to myself,' and explained, 'I had this conservatory in my house – three steps went up to kind of a raised part of our kitchen. I used it as the stage.' With a smile, he added, 'My mum was trying to cook and I was pretending I was at the O2 Arena.'

Subsequently, with continued practice, Sam's own singing style began to evolve. 'I trained as hard as I could and sang the highest songs I could sing,' he told *Vibe*, 'I think Mariah [Carey] brought out a record during that time and I just sang it every day.' Soon he began pushing his upper range, determined to replicate the higher, female singing voices he idolised, until he could sing along with Whitney and Chaka, as well as Mariah, matching them note for note. 'For me, it's always been normal, I could always sing high,' he told BBC News, before admitting he had become obsessed with pushing his voice to its upper limit to mimic his favourite singers, adding, 'I wanted to hit the notes they were hitting.'

Soon, he had developed a fairly impressive vocal range and his repertoire of songs expanded accordingly. 'I used to love singing Norah Jones because her voice was low enough and I could really go for it.' He admitted he'd even attempted to master a few Britney Spears numbers, before acknowledging, 'but that was when my voice wasn't broken.' His emerging talent for singing hadn't gone unnoticed, with both his parents recognising something special, even at such an early stage. 'I was eight years old and my parents thought I could sing,' Sam told *The New York Times*. 'So they put me into singing lessons with a local jazz teacher.'

That singing tutor was Joanna Eden, a respected jazz musician, who just happened to live in nearby Saffron Walden. Eden had been born into a musical family, encouraged to play piano from the age of six, and had eventually studied creative arts in Manchester. She began her professional career as a singer/pianist playing venues in London's Soho, before forming a jazz group with her drummer husband, Charlie Price, and guitarist Dan Boutwood. As a trio they performed on cruise liners, travelling extensively around the world, before Eden and Price returned to the UK in the late 1990s and settled in Cambridgeshire. After releasing one critically acclaimed album, *A Little Bird Told Me*, in 2000, Eden went into semi-retirement, temporarily quitting her recording career to focus on starting a family.

During this period she decided to offer her professional services as a singing teacher and she was first introduced to Sam Smith. Eden would soon become a very important influence on his singing style and song repertoire. She quickly went from simply being his tutor to being a valued mentor and over the next few years their relationship evolved even further. Eventually, singing alongside Eden would give Sam his first experiences of performing onstage as a professional musician and over time, their bond developed into a genuine, long-lasting friendship.

To begin with, Sam's parents had arranged for him to see Eden once a week. 'I remember our first lesson,' he recalled in an interview with *Fader*. 'I sang Frank Sinatra's "Come Fly With Me" and "Get Happy" by Judy Garland.' While he was hardly shy about singing in front of his family, performing for an 'outsider' was a relatively new experience. 'You know when your parents say you are good at something? You are like, "Yeah, whatever",' he explained. 'But when the teacher said, "You've got something here" – I had never received a compliment for anything, because I was always quite average.'

Although Sam's parents had always been the first to champion their son's talent, urging him to take it seriously and trying to boost his confidence, hearing positive feedback from a professional singer was obviously something altogether more rewarding. In an interview with the *Telegraph*, Eden described her first impressions of Sam, saying, 'I had never taught a boy before but his dad said, "We think he's got a really good voice". At the end of the lesson I said, "He's extraordinary".'

Eden heard something unique and was immediately on board to offer support and encouragement. She later recalled, 'He just had the most powerful voice, with great control and also the courage to try stuff.' Eden's praise, it would seem, was all Sam needed to commit further to learning how to professionally train his voice and fully exploit its potential. 'For someone to hear my voice and be like, "Wow",' he admitted to *Fader*, 'I really fed off that.' His reaction was instantaneous and all-consuming. 'As soon as I realised I was good at it,' he confessed to *The New York Times*, 'I ran with it, and haven't really stopped since.'

As these lessons progressed, Eden would help Sam to fully exploit his full vocal range, enhancing the skills he'd already started to develop on his own. Most importantly, she taught Sam how to look after his voice, helping him to avoid the devastating issues that can arise when untrained singers push their vocal chords to the extremes he was attempting to reach. By helping him to acknowledge his limitations and respect the natural boundaries he was already attempting to push through, Sam was developing his own style, cultivating his unique tone and becoming a much more intelligent and nuanced singer.

By the age of ten, Sam's life was already beginning to revolve almost completely around his new passion. His time was now devoted more or less completely to either singing or listening to music. Obsessed, he never stopped wanting to explore further and deeper into the world of singers and the songs they were singing. If he wasn't at Eden's lessons, he was practising in the car or at home. Sam meticulously studied the techniques of his favourite artists as he listened to their songs through headphones, taking walks in the nearby villages or sitting in isolated spots in the surrounding countryside.

When asked by CBS News if he remembered Sam as a boy, Jim Cunningham, a neighbour from Great Chishill, recalled,

'Yeah, of course I do. He used to knock around here causing all kinds of trouble and he used to be screeching out of that window up there,' before adding, 'But it was wonderful.' Maybe not the best live review Sam's ever received, but it demonstrates the growing confidence he now had about performing in front of others and in public.

Indeed Sam was more than happy to provide the entertainment whenever there was a family gathering or friends visited the house. It would seem Kate had developed a passion for hosting get-togethers at home, and whether it was a group of familiar faces, or a roomful of his mother's work colleagues and business associates, Sam would climb the steps to the raised platform in the conservatory (which acted as a makeshift stage) and sing his heart out.

'Whenever my mum had dinner parties and when she was drunk, she used to make me go up on the stage and sing to everyone,' he told *Fader*, adding that after he'd made a half-hearted protest, 'I did, for some absurd reason.' It has to be said, the reason was fairly obvious… Sam undoubtedly loved the attention. But it wasn't just his singing he was keen to show off – it would seem he'd already caught the 'performance bug' and was willing to turn anything into a show. He told the *Telegraph*, 'If someone was talking about a subject, Mum would be like, "Oh, that happened to us last week. Sam, tell everyone".' He added, 'At ten years old that is quite daunting, to chat to a whole table of adults and hold your own. There's an art to it.' While he would later admit these early experiences made him unusually confident, perhaps putting 'an old head on my shoulders', he was adamant this level-headedness would prove to be extremely beneficial in the future, stressing, 'I'd never want to lose that.'

By the time he turned eleven, Sam was starting to take singing and performing even more seriously. He had bought a mini amplifier and it seemed that performing in front of a few drunken party guests was no longer enough to satisfy his needs. Sam craved the opportunity to sing for real audiences and his emerging talent for holding court was in need of more formal nurturing. Soon he was enrolled as a member of the Saffron Walden Amateur Operatic Society's junior section and he began to flourish in this enthusiastic and prolific company.

When he eventually moved from his primary school in Saffron Walden to St Mary's secondary school, a good ten miles further away in Bishop's Stortford, Hertfordshire, it made sense for Sam to join the local amateur dramatics group there. As a member of Bishop's Stortford Musical Theatre Society, he began to meet a few people who were not only around his own age but who shared his passion for singing and performing. It was here Sam formed some important and long-lasting friendships, including becoming close friends with Beth Rowe, who would become one of his flatmates almost a decade later when he moved to London.

Sam told *Interview* magazine that however much he enjoyed taking part in the shows he didn't always take it as seriously as he should have. 'Me and my best friend Beth were in all the musicals together and we were really badly behaved,' he admitted. 'So they just put us in the back.' Perhaps it had more to do with this mischievous side of his character than any lack of singing ability or charisma but

Sam admits to being completely overlooked as a lead in any of the shows he was involved in, spending most of his time merely as part of the chorus. He would later tell BBC News there was a definite 'pecking order' in terms of who got the bigger roles and the opportunity to step into the limelight never came.

During his time there, the company staged a wide variety of productions, including well-known Broadway musicals such as *42nd Street*, *Oklahoma*, *The Sound of Music* and *Annie Get Your Gun*, as well as putting together several cabaret concerts. Lack of star-billing aside, he enjoyed the feeling of being a part of something and never tired of getting up on stage, admitting to BBC News, 'One time I did six shows in one year, while juggling school.' Perhaps most notable among the productions Sam took part in was a kids'-only version of *The Rocky Horror Show*, something his school friend (and future roommate) Tiffany Clare described to *Rolling Stone* as 'the talk of the town.'

As time passed, Sam began diversifying even further. As well as learning jazz from Joanna Eden and exploring the world of musical theatre, he would become a member of the renowned Cantate Youth Choir. Formed in 1996, the Bishop's Stortford-based choir has since gone on to achieve international acclaim, having successfully competed in countless competition events around the world. The choir's songbook was extensive and undeniably eclectic, with their joint musical director, Nicholas Shaw, telling the *Herts and Essex Observer* that the choir's members could expect to be 'singing *West Side Story* and Schumann in the same breath.' Shaw stated, 'It is all about singing a quality repertoire well, really working at something to take it into the realms of excellence,' insisting that being a part of the choir not only exposed the young singers to music they might never have heard before, but also provided a valuable life lesson.

Here, as part of the choir, Sam would have learned the importance of teamwork and pulling together to achieve something special, as well as gaining an early insight into how much effort was actually involved in achieving any degree of meaningful success. While it's true the youngsters in the choir were expected to push themselves, it wasn't all hard work, though. Aside from instilling a solid work ethic, the choir encouraged its members to take pride in their achievements and, most of all, have fun.

Sam's confidence was growing and it wasn't long before he wanted to step out on his own. He began booking solo gigs and was soon performing at local events, including one memorable appearance at a local barn dance. 'I had to sing on this stage on top of a haystack,' he told GQ. 'And I had to sing to backing tracks for an hour and a half while everyone was pissed,' concluding, 'I didn't know the words: it was awful.'

It would seem he was learning the hard way that singing professionally was not all glamour and endless applause. He was becoming fairly well known in his local area, with his appearances as part of the youth theatre group and the Cantate Choir, as well as an eagerness to take to the stage at every possible opportunity, and so it was hardly a surprise when he began to get noticed a little further afield. Outside parties were beginning to express an interest in managing Sam's career and everyone seemed to agree that a 'strike while the iron is hot' approach was in order.

With his extracurricular activities taking up so much of his free time, Sam was an extraordinarily busy young man but he liked it that way. While he tended not to worry too much about the added pressure he was putting himself under – pursuing his passion for singing while studying for exams at school – Sam was beginning to feel uncharacteristically uneasy and suffered crippling bouts of anxiety. 'As early as twelve years old, I used to have panic attacks,' he confessed to *GQ*, 'because I needed to know my life plan.' He was indeed at a crossroads – several avenues were opening up to him in terms of where his singing would take him, and his ambition to succeed made him impatient and keen to move on to the next challenge. But however eager he was to take his career to the next level, there was no getting away from the fact that he was still a young boy and the extra pressure he was experiencing was a lot for anyone to deal with, especially for someone as sensitive as Sam.

He often attributes this side of his character to the predominately female influence exerted on him as a child. Indeed, he had been brought up in a household where powerful women ruled the roost and any influence exerted by his father was less domineering and more nurturing. 'The guys are amazing in our family,' he told *Fader*, 'but they are more feminine. The females are the providers.'

Despite Sam's dad, Fred, casting a constant and influential shadow over his childhood, it was his mum Kate, eventually joined by his two sisters, who really set the tone around the house. The effect this had on the young Sam was fairly profound. 'I'm a highly emotional person,' he admitted to *The Line of Best Fit*. 'I think if you spoke to my mum, she will tell you that I've been that emotional since I was twelve years old.' But he had benefited from growing up in this atmosphere of openness and acceptance, learning to express himself fully without fear of rejection or judgement. 'My family always wears their hearts on their sleeves,' he admitted. 'If we're feeling something, we tell each other.'

Like most young men on the cusp of their teens, Sam was also coming to terms with the hormonal upheaval that inevitably goes hand in hand with entering adolescence. But unlike the other boys in his class, who were experiencing the expected outbreak of spots, growth spurts and the inexplicable urge to consume and discuss at great length every minute detail of every single episode of *The Inbetweeners*, he was wrestling with something altogether more complicated. Sam had spent years quietly contemplating the question of his sexuality, coming to the conclusion that it wasn't something he needed to worry too much about. He had long since accepted that he was simply 'different' without ever having to label it or discuss it with others. Whether he had always known he was gay, or if it was just a general feeling of 'not quite fitting in', he insists it was never an issue in his own mind.

'I've always been an open book about it,' he would eventually reveal to the *Telegraph*. 'This was a constant thing: I came out as a gay man at a very, very young age.' Indeed, he says he never really had to officially 'come out' to his family, insisting they'd always known and his parents more or less guessed from when he was a toddler. 'My mum said she knew when I was like three,' Sam confessed on Ellen DeGeneres' US chat show, before joking, 'I came out when I was like four years old!'

But now, as he hit puberty, it was definitely becoming more of an issue among his friends and more specifically with the other boys at school. Sam had always felt slightly isolated from the boys in his class. He was never invited into their gangs and felt much more comfortable making friends with the girls in his year. While he took part in some sports – he enjoyed swimming, was a fairly keen tennis player and did gymnastics at school – he had virtually no interest in football or the other team games that seemed to unite most of the boys of his age. Though he felt completely removed from most of the things the boys in his class talked about, he never felt the need to pretend just to fit in.

Music might be considered a great leveller, an obvious subject for teenagers to bond over, but Sam's almost exclusive interest in female divas and soul music invariably set him apart. There was no way he was going to get the emotional intensity he required from his favourite singers from the bands most of his male classmates were listening to. In his mind Whitney Houston, Celine Dion and Mariah Carey triumphed over The Killers, Franz Ferdinand and Green Day any day of the week.

Sam has described his coming out to friends at this time as a need to be completely honest about who he was rather than any particular need for acceptance. By then he had definitely developed his own (some might say unique) sense of style. Often he wore make-up and at one point, when he was in Year 11, dyed his hair bright red, although he admits it was more 'plumy purple'.

Sam had come to understand being gay was something completely natural. He'd grown up with it and insisted it wasn't something to hide or to be ashamed of. But he was equally keen on his privacy, adamant that being a gay man wasn't how he wanted to define himself. So, those who'd found out about his sexuality by this point had probably guessed and, as far as Sam was concerned, those who hadn't obviously didn't really need to know.

But the reality wasn't quite so simple. Sam and his family lived in a relatively small village. It was the kind of place where everyone knew everyone else's business and if people wanted to gossip, there wasn't really anything anyone could do to stop them. At school, Sam's sexuality was generally accepted by the students he thought of as his closest friends; even outside that small group, he felt it had never really been too much of an issue.

When he was about thirteen years old, a classmate approached him and asked him bluntly if he was gay. Sam recalled in *Rolling Stone*, 'I turned 'round, and I was just like, "Yeah",' before adding, 'Everything changed.' While he wouldn't experience anything that could be described as overtly homophobic abuse or physical attacks at school, he remembers countless small, more indirect incidents, which did upset him. He remembered borrowing an eraser from one of his fellow students, only to watch him wash it after he'd returned it. Sam explained, 'He was like, "I don't want to share my eraser with a gay man."'

Sam admits that a couple of years later he sent what he now describes as a 'really intense' love letter to a boy who studied at the same school, but was two years older. The boy was considered one of the more popular kids. Sam had singled him out because he seemed artistic and he thought they might share some of the same interests. The boy turned out to be straight, but rather than ridiculing Sam, or rejecting him in a cruel way, he wrote him a lengthy, thoughtful reply, explaining he only thought of Sam as a friend.

Looking back at the incident recently, Sam admitted, 'It makes me emotional,' before explaining, 'He looked out for me for the rest of school. He just made sure that if anyone took the piss out of me, he would stick up for me. He could have made it hell for me.'

Unfortunately, outside the shelter of the school gates, away from the protection of his 'guardian angel', Sam faced a more challenging situation. Not everyone in the village was as comfortable with his sexuality. There were obvious disadvantages that went with being known as the only openly gay teen in the community and Sam became an easy target for some of the more narrow-minded residents. 'I felt isolated,' he confessed to the *London Evening Standard*. 'I was called "faggot" many times.' He went on to recall, 'I worked part-time in a shop. There was a man in the village who had a massive issue with me being gay and didn't want me serving him.' While this obviously made Sam uneasy, he had been dealing with the everyday complexities involved with accepting his own sexuality for such a long time that it wasn't something he took too much to heart. However, when the abuse impacted on other members of his family, he was considerably less comfortable. On one occasion when he was walking through the village with his dad, someone drove past them shouting 'Faggot!' out of the car window. Sam told *Rolling Stone*, 'I was just embarrassed that my dad had to see that, because I could only imagine how you feel as a parent,' and then added, 'You just want to kill them. I was embarrassed for the people around me. It never deeply affected me.' Even in his early teens, Sam's strength of character and determination to 'be himself' would become a driving force in his future career.

It was in this state of mind that Sam began to really focus on his long-term future. He'd spent a long time daydreaming about what it would be like to achieve the same level of success as his idols, but now he had to get serious. He realised he had a lot to learn and there were some big decisions to make about the people who would help him reach his ultimate goal. Sam has spoken candidly about the fact he had several different managers before he had even left school. As news started to spread about this young singer with a uniquely powerful voice, it's hardly surprising that he would attract the attention of individuals keen to nurture his talent.

While it's safe to say not everyone Sam encountered during this period had his best interests at heart, it was equally true he would need professional help if he wanted to move his career on to the next level. Thus, over the next few years, he would make deals with several artist managers, each with a different view on which direction his career should progress.

It was undoubtedly an unsettling period. He was barely a teenager, trying to juggle school work and all his extra singing activities, and there is no doubt he was putting himself under a great deal of pressure. But amid the stories of false starts and disappointments, Sam was receiving some very valuable lessons. Through these managers he was finally meeting industry professionals and talent agents who knew exactly how the music industry operated and how difficult it was to build and maintain a successful recording career. He now had professional help to arrange bigger and more prestigious gigs, and it was during this time that he would make his first tentative steps into songwriting and recording his own music. It didn't always work out exactly as he wanted it to, but there's no denying it was firing Sam's hunger to succeed and giving him a taste of what life as a successful recording artist could be like.

CHAPTER TWO

ROCKY ROAD

'There will always be people who will try to use anyone for whatever they can get, but I think I'm wise enough, even at 16, to keep away from those people.'
Sam Smith on finding a safe passage through the music industry –
Bent Magazine, April 2009

The music industry, like any business reliant on making a profit from the creativity and craft of others, can be a difficult environment for the artists themselves to navigate. Countless stories have emerged over the years of aspiring musicians, writers and filmmakers struggling to make it over the very first hurdle. In a moment of sheer desperation, they effectively sign their lives away and agree to do almost anything in an attempt to get their foot in the door. It's an unavoidable truth that many of those artists never make it, and it's an even more inevitable fact that the ones who do will have found the experience traumatic. An artist relies on the professionals they've employed to protect them, promote them or simply guide them through the veritable maze of planning, deals and contracts necessary to keep them in business. However, these relationships often break down, sometimes with significant fallout.

In 1985, Elton John and Bernie Taupin successfully sued Dick James Music, the company run by the man who'd given them their first publishing deal, for unpaid royalties on hundreds of songs they had written. They failed in their claim for copyright for over 150 of the songs they'd written under the contract, songs which would have earned them an estimated £200 million in sales over the intervening years.

George Michael's first record deal, in the early days of Wham!, was with independent label Innervision Records. It was described by former Dire Straits manager, Ed Bicknell, in the *Independent* in October 1993 as 'an all out turkey' and 'worse than not having a deal at all'. Wham! managed to leave Innervision, and in early 1984 signed with Epic, part of major label CBS. But even after an impressive run of Top 10 singles and No.1 albums with Wham! and as a solo artist, by the 1990s, Michael felt unhappy about this second contract, by which time CBS was part of Sony Music. Again, Bicknell commented, 'For someone of his calibre, it's a shit deal,' before adding, 'I've got an unknown on my books who's got a better deal than George Michael.' Hoping to free himself from his Sony contract, Michael famously fought (and lost) his case in the High Court in June 1994, which resulted in a potentially disastrous extended recording hiatus and a six-year gap between his last Sony album, *Listen Without Prejudice, Vol. 1*, and his first album under his new deal with Virgin Records, *Older*.

Artist management is a very competitive business and virtually every young band or singer has a story to tell. For someone as young as Sam, and with parents who had no prior experience of the music industry, it was a daunting prospect.

For Sam was in a fairly unique proposition. As a pre-teen singer with an extraordinary range and power in his voice, there was definitely a lot of interest in trying to find the right angle to entice quality producers and the big record labels to work with him or sign him to a deal. 'I had a lot of adults around me and they could see something,' he admitted to the *Telegraph*. 'But I don't think they knew what to do with it.' It was a time he now describes as 'tough', but if there was a positive spin to focus on, it was the fact that plenty of people out there in the 'real world' recognised that he did indeed possess a special talent.

Thankfully, despite the pressure which must have been on him to commit to singing full-time, Sam never considered dropping out of school as an option, realising very early on how precarious his chosen career could be and knowing the value in having some decent qualifications to fall back on. Through all this, his parents were always on hand to act as the voice of reason. Sam was in no doubt that whenever there was a major setback, he was surrounded by people who really cared for him. His parents strived to keep his feet on the ground and steered him through any difficult decisions that had to be made. With several outside parties recognising he had potential (even if they were a little unsure exactly how to nurture it) and his dependable, family support system in place, things were definitely looking up. But as Sam reached puberty, like every other boy his age, there was an unavoidable and inevitable change waiting just around the corner.

Talking to *Vibe*, he confessed, 'I was so sad when my mum and dad told me that my balls were gonna drop.' He admitted, 'When they told me my voice was gonna break, I remember nearly crying and going crazy.' Similarly, he told *NPR*, 'I used to get very angry as I was getting older, because my voice was breaking.' Indeed, it was a frustrating time for him, but eventually he understood it was a natural obstacle every young male singer must face. As difficult as it was, he was reassured by the fact it was likely he'd come out the other side with a different, but equally powerful voice. And in the end, as it seemed to be whenever he faced any obstacle which stood between him and his dream of becoming a professional singer, it only made him all the more determined to succeed.

Reluctant to abandon the extensive vocal range he had developed over the last few years, Sam worked tirelessly to train his voice even harder. Nothing was going to stop him reclaiming the high notes he'd previously reached so effortlessly, while singing along to the likes of Whitney and Mariah in the years before his voice broke. 'I wanted to be able to hit the notes that those females hit,' he later confessed. 'So I've trained my voice so religiously through my teenage years.' He started to push himself even more, and now with Joanna Eden's professional help and guidance, he was soon at the point where he was once again able to replicate the voices of his female idols, comfortably reaching the extremes of their vocal ranges and matching their control and versatility. 'It does come naturally,' he explained, 'but I also work at it. I try to make it look like it's effortless, but it's not.' He added: 'That's the same for anyone, you know? You look at runners in the Olympics, and watch the way they run. You think, "I can do that." Uh, you can't.'

He now possessed an even more unusual gift. While most young male singers who've had formal voice training as children might be expected to be able to hit some fairly impressive high notes before their voices break, to continue to hit them as a teenager, and then as an adult, was something else entirely. With his voice now broken, any uncertainty surrounding Sam being able to maintain his full vocal power and range when it settled was well and truly over. Still in his teens, he was now in the enviable position of being able to weigh up several career options and start mapping out his future with more certainty.

While still heavily involved with musical theatre, it was obvious he was never going to be a leading player within the group. Although he seemed content to sing as part of the company, simply enjoying the experience and having fun with his friends, it was only a matter of time before Sam outgrew performing as part of the Bishop's Stortford Youth Theatre chorus.

Simultaneously, it seems he was learning more and more about stage craft and performance from Joanna Eden, joining her on stage as one of her backing singers at several professional gigs. This was undoubtedly helping to build his confidence, but it also seems to have given him a taste of what it was like to really hold the attention of an audience. Eden was showing him exactly what he could achieve, simply by performing his own songs and sharing the power of his voice with an audience. Slowly, he seemed to be coming to a decision about his future on his own, but it was obvious he needed time to weigh up all his options and choose the correct path.

Ever the optimist, it would seem he was determined to grit his teeth and make the best of a bad situation. Having already accepted he needed guidance, Sam decided to try and take on board every bit of advice he was offered. Hopefully, he reasoned, he'd come out the other side wiser and suitably prepared for whatever the future had to throw at him. It would seem he was simply putting on a brave face.

As time went on, as Sam continued to try and figure out what type of singer he wanted to be, things were not going smoothly. As managers came and went, he was becoming increasingly frustrated. No two managers shared the same vision as to which direction his music career should take and Sam tried concentrating on singing other people's songs, re-interpreting old standards and popular jazz tunes, like a (considerably younger) Michael Bublé, in an attempt to attract a more mature audience. Sam undoubtedly understood the appeal of Michael Bublé and respected him as an artist, but he must have also been conscious that, at that point in his career at least, Bublé was best known for singing covers whereas Sam himself was increasingly keen to start writing and recording his own, original material. So he was understandably disheartened. While he loved the classics, and there was no doubt he could definitely sing such songs, his real passion was for pop and something with a little more soul.

Even when things seemed to be going well and Sam's career was finally gaining some traction, it would often feel like one step forward and three steps back. 'There were a lot of false promises,' he recalled in the *Guardian*. 'I was told, "It's all going to kick off for you next year"' – and inevitably, it didn't. It was a vicious circle, which was slowly grinding Sam down. He told *Fader*, 'When I was fourteen or fifteen, I was promised stardom ... I was thinking, "Great, I can leave school at sixteen."' Of course he couldn't wait to share his good fortune with his friends. He recalled, 'I'd go to school the next day and I'd be like, "I'm going to be doing this in a few months, I'm going to be singing a song with this person." It never materialised, and I looked like a complete idiot.'

During this particularly frustrating period, it would seem his parents were eager to regain at least a small degree of control over their son's future. Keen to get Sam's career back on more solid ground, Fred and Kate were always there to offer support in any way they could and were more than willing to take matters into their own hands, if necessary. They were constantly on the lookout for suitable opportunities that could potentially lead to a breakthrough for their son's career.

So, when Kate saw an advert asking for singers and musicians to come forward to take part in a local talent competition, *South Coast Idol*, it seemed ideal. She immediately showed it to Sam, suggesting he should just go along and see what happened. However, it would seem he had already made up his mind about auditioning for televised talent competitions such as *The X Factor* and *Britain's Got Talent*. When asked if he had any desire to appear on this type of show, he emphatically told the local Chishill Newsletter, 'No, unless I was desperate!'

It seems likely his obvious distaste for Simon Cowell's

brand of instant stardom, and his rejection of the apparent overnight success it promised, was at least partly motivated by the fact that, at only fifteen years of age at the time, he probably assumed he was still too young to enter *The X Factor* audition process. But, while *The X Factor* had maintained a lower age limit of sixteen for its first three years, the fourth and fifth seasons controversially saw the minimum age limit lowered even further. Ironically, 2007 – the year Sam celebrated his fifteenth birthday – was the very year the age range was temporarily lowered and singers as young as fourteen years old were now eligible to apply.

But there was obviously more than mere age restrictions behind Sam's contempt: the type of instant and widespread celebrity generated by shows like *The X Factor* was undeniably useful to anyone hoping to achieve success as a singer or in a group, but for anyone hoping to build a credible career, based on real talent and with any degree of longevity, it was something of a double-edged sword.

James Merritt, a successful radio DJ and founder of artist management company, Authority MGMT, who has helped nurture the early careers of artists such as Ella Eyre (a future Brit Award nominee alongside Sam), recently discussed the issues involved in this type of high-profile launch. Merritt explained to the *Guardian*, 'With *The X Factor* there is massive exposure for the artists so they're already known to the public when they put their music out.' He went on to say he'd purposely avoided this particular route for launching the artists in his charge. 'If you're dealing with more of an organic artist, such as Ella [Eyre], then there has to be some way of getting her name known without running the risk that if you put the first single out and it doesn't work that she'll be labelled as a flop.' He concluded: 'You want to make sure that she's getting out there but without actually risking too much.'

As Sam's own career aspirations were beginning to come into focus, and he was slowly developing a picture of what type of artist he could eventually become, he realised he wanted to be creatively involved, at every level, with the music he made. He had started to make his first tentative steps into songwriting and while he realised he had a long way to go, his first attempts pushed him to keep exploring and perfecting his own style of writing. It would appear, even at this early stage, Sam's growing interest in developing his songwriting skills was fuelled in part by his desire to have more control over his future musical output. If success finally came his way, he had no desire to become a virtual puppet on a reality TV talent show and watch his artistic freedom and long-term career goals go up in smoke.

In some respects, his decision to apply, and eventually take part in, *South Coast Idol* seems slightly at odds with even his earliest aspirations to become a credible recording artist. But, in terms of giving him local media exposure and valuable performance experience in front of a live audience, it was an undeniably useful opportunity. As he would later acknowledge, there were multiple occasions during those early stages of his career when he grew increasingly desperate to do whatever it took to get his big break. Willing to do anything to break the cycle of raised expectations and the crushing disappointments that inevitably followed, perhaps this could be seen as the first obvious example of the immense pressure Sam was exerting on himself to succeed, and clear evidence of the ambitious nature he'd inherited from his mother. There was no denying a competition like this was something that would raise his profile, even if it wasn't exactly what he thought he should be doing and, ultimately, there was little to lose just by taking part.

In the end, maybe taking part in *South Coast Idol* offered him a comfortable middle ground. He got the publicity boost and a taste of what it was like to take part in this type of singing competition, but as it was a non-televised event, and therefore slightly lower profile in terms of the national media, the stakes were considerably lower. For Sam, at this point, there seemed to be more to gain and virtually nothing to lose.

South Coast Idol started as a regional music talent competition in the South of England before eventually becoming affiliated with *Live and Unsigned*, a much more comprehensive search to find the best undiscovered music acts from around the UK. Winners from the regional heats would eventually perform together at a Grand Final, where the ultimate winner would be offered a management deal, a recording contract with a £20,000 advance and the opportunity to work with established music producers and songwriters.

Initially open only to unsigned singers and bands over the age of seventeen, the competition had grown considerably since its launch in 2005. Having attracted close to 5,000 applicants in its second year, the organisers were now receiving an exceptional number of requests to fall in line with ITV's *The X Factor* and opened the competition to younger applicants. Thus, when the competition returned for a third year, now fully under the *Live and Unsigned* umbrella, it had been decided there was indeed sufficient demand to warrant expanding their search for new artists even further, opting to hold more auditions than in previous years and including extra categories. Thus, the required minimum age had been lowered and a new Under-17s category was introduced in a move that saw applications more than double. So, with over 10,000 hopefuls wishing to audition, *Live and Unsigned* had quickly become the UK's second biggest music contest behind *The X Factor*.

While there were obvious similarities with Simon Cowell's TV-ratings juggernaut, especially with an increased focus on younger contestants, the two competitions seemed to serve a very different purpose. *The X Factor* has undoubtedly produced several noteworthy contestants but while artists such as Leona Lewis, JLS, Olly Murs and One Direction have enjoyed sustained success on leaving the show, others have found it harder in the real world and trying to forge a career in the music industry. What began as a genuine search for talented singers has become primarily an entertainment show and, more evident in recent years, delivering a large Saturday night TV audience seems to have taken precedence over discovering great singers or artists possessing true creativity or longevity.

Live and Unsigned organiser and co-founder Chris Grayston was adamant the intent of their show was completely different. 'This cannot be compared to *X Factor*,' he told the *Royston Crow*. 'We encourage contestants to do their own thing, whether that be their own genre, style, play their own instruments or perform their own songs.' In the years since its launch, *Live and Unsigned* had established itself as a breeding ground for new artists. It was now attracting the attention of talent agents, artist managers and scouts for record company A&R departments, while becoming a unique platform for young artists hoping to showcase their skills as performers, songwriters and musicians.

Singer-songwriter Jasmine van den Bogaerde, who performs under the name Birdy, was discovered after winning *Live and Unsigned*'s affiliated *Open Mic UK* competition at the age of twelve, eventually signing a deal with Warner Music when she was just fourteen years old, and has since released two internationally successful albums. It would seem this freer approach appealed to Sam and he decided to apply to *Live and Unsigned*, telling his local newspaper, 'I went there thinking, just give it a go.' It would prove to be a very shrewd move. Taking part in the competition would put his voice centre-stage, giving him far greater exposure than the local events and musical theatre productions he'd taken part in over the last few years. And perhaps more importantly, *Live and Unsigned* would hopefully put him on the radar of some well-connected artist managers, music producers or industry insiders – anyone who could help him make his real break into the music business.

In early 2007, when the first auditions took place, Sam was still only fourteen years old. But as someone who had been singing constantly for the previous five or six years, and whose confidence had benefited from appearing in several shows with the Bishop's Stortford Youth Theatre, he could almost be considered a veteran performer. More than ready to take the stage, he wasn't going to let nerves get the better of him and he managed to make quite an impression during the early stages of the elimination process. Indeed, he seemed to handle the added pressure with ease, sailing through his first audition and was suitably well prepared for the next round of eliminations.

As the competition continued, those contestants who successfully made it through three regional heats were expected to perform in front of a live audience, as well as the panel of music industry experts and celebrity judges. In order to advance further, Sam needed to prove he was much more than a just a decent karaoke singer; he had to show he had the necessary skills to entertain a crowd. Consisting largely of family members and close friends who'd come along to support and cheer for the other contestants, it certainly wasn't going to be the easiest crowd he would ever sing for. But for someone his age, Sam's vocal power was undeniable. Coupled with his growing confidence and natural charisma, his progress to the next round was almost inevitable.

Sam delivered stunning versions of Whitney Houston's 'My Love is Your Love' and Nina Simone's 'Feeling Good' in his heats, which saw him safely through to compete at the Grand Final. As always, his parents were on hand to show their support and at the last semi-final, his father was particularly emotional. 'When they called his name out as best male it was a very moving moment,' Fred told the *Herts and Essex Observer*. 'We're very proud of him,' and then added, 'But at the same time we're not the sort of people to get carried away.' This last statement is particularly telling. Despite how it might have appeared from the outside, Fred and Kate were far from the clichéd 'Pushy Stage Mum and

Dad'. While they were the first to encourage Sam to follow his passion for singing, they would have been equally supportive had their son developed an interest in science or more academic pursuits. Ultimately, they had no desire to make Sam do anything he didn't want to do and, as non-musicians, there was no element of him fulfilling any of their own missed opportunities or making up for their own artistic aspirations.

Over the last couple of years there had been a great deal of upheaval in Sam's life, in terms of who was supposed to be advising his parents on which route they should take to make the most of his talents and planning ahead for his future. But it's safe to say Kate and Fred remained steadfast in their unwavering belief in his talent and were a constant source of support. With their help, Sam never lost faith. He remained refreshingly optimistic, buoyed by growing confidence and an ambitious streak that never allowed him to imagine failure. Despite the numerous knock-backs and disappointments, his impatience to succeed was stronger than ever.

As the *Live and Unsigned* final approached, he was justifiably proud of his achievement so far and excited about the opportunities which were slowly opening up to him. Sam, and everyone around him, was convinced his determination was finally paying off, even if everything wasn't moving along quite at the pace he himself wanted it to. If nothing else, his progression through the different stages of the competition was proof indeed that his voice was enough to secure the future he'd started to dream about. There were no tricks or gimmicks; no magic solutions or quick fixes. No manager or agent could take credit for what was happening here, it was Sam's voice and his skills as a singer that were winning over the crowds and impressing the judges.

Suddenly, things were finally moving in the right direction, and with a seemingly unstoppable forward momentum. It would appear Sam was slowly beginning to realise his voice was the only vital component which would secure his future success and while he accepted he'd need help to get there, he would insist he had some control over his own destiny. With this attitude firmly in place things were definitely looking up, even before the final took place.

The increased exposure Sam had already gained from the competition led to another team of managers expressing an interest in taking his career to the next level. Sam felt this team were on the right wavelength, intent on guiding him towards an end goal which matched his own ideas of how he wanted to progress. Sam's dad, Fred, told the *Herts and Essex Observer*: 'A management company which loves Sam's voice are funding a studio visit for him. They've given him three songs to play around with. If they like the results, they'll send them round to some big record companies.' Finally, just as Sam seemed to be getting a clearer idea of the type of artist he wanted to be, he'd met a team who appeared to share his vision and it's safe to imagine he was beginning to think the long periods of indecision and doubt about his future were coming to an end.

The *Live and Unsigned* Grand Final took place on 26 May 2007 at the Portsmouth Guildhall. Sam was one of eighteen semi-finalists competing across several different categories, with only the overall winner taking away the big prize of a management deal and a £20,000 recording advance. The winner was decided by a combination of votes from a judging panel and the audience, with other factors – such as how many press clippings each contestant had managed to amass during the course of the competition and how many final tickets they'd managed to sell to their friends and family – also having an impact on the final outcome.

While hardly in the same league as *The X Factor* Finale at London's O2 or Wembley's SSE Arena, *Live and Unsigned* was big enough to attract a few celebrities to perform on the same bill as the contestants, with a re-formed East 17, *X Factor* runner-up Ben Mills and former Atomic Kitten member, Liz McClarnon, all taking to the stage that night. Similarly, the judging panel was a little less star-studded than the average televised talent show, but did include a few credible music industry insiders – among them record producer Mark Hill, the man responsible for turning Craig David's debut album, *Born to Do It*, into a multi-platinum success, Lee Latchford-Evans (from the pop group Steps), choreographer Tim Noble, who had worked with the likes of Kylie Minogue and Girls Aloud, and Katie Holmes, a respected vocal coach and part-time backing singer.

Momentarily abandoning his almost exclusive repertoire of female divas, Sam had chosen to perform John Legend's song 'Ordinary People' in the final. In the end, despite giving a noteworthy performance, it wasn't quite enough for him to scoop the main prize. Instead, sixteen-year-old Francesca 'Fizz' Reynolds took the top award after playing keyboards and singing one of her own compositions, with Sam taking the runner-up spot. It would seem he lost out due to the competition's emphasis on singers who played instruments, and also wrote their own songs. While he must have been disappointed about the end result, though, losing only seemed to put a fire in his belly and he was more determined than ever to start writing and recording more of his own material. Keen to fully exploit the added interest stirred up by the exposure *Live and Unsigned* had generated, he was moving forward with his plans to record some songs given to him by his latest management team.

It's fairly ironic that in recent years competitions such as *Live and Unsigned* have become increasingly important in unearthing talented youngsters who go on to do well in shows such as *The X Factor* and *The Voice*. It's believed to be common practice for talent scouts associated with these shows to earmark singers who have done well in *Live and Unsigned* (or its affiliated competitions, *Open Mic UK* and *Teen Star*) and sign them up for 'priority' auditions. Contestants such as Luke Friend, Lucy Spraggan and Union J's Jaymi Hensley have all made it to *The X Factor* live shows after reaching various stages in recent *Live and Unsigned* competitions. Whether or not this was an option for Sam is unclear but it's safe to say he had his eye on a bigger prize.

In the couple of months immediately after the competition, Sam was busier than ever and it was clear something had to give. Of course, while all this was going on, he was still at school, preparing to take his GCSEs. While juggling studies with trying to launch a full-time singing career might have been virtually impossible for anyone else, he never shied away from the hectic schedule and long hours which made it possible.

But it wasn't only Sam who was feeling the extra pressure. The recent developments in his singing career put new demands on the whole Smith family. His parents were expected to pick him up from school in the evenings and deliver him to wherever he needed to be. Whereas before it might be a meeting with another prospective manager or his regular singing lesson with Eden, now it could mean long round trips to a London recording studio, all of which had to fit in with the rest of the family's busy timetables. It was tiring and time-consuming, especially as Sam had two younger sisters with similarly hectic school and social lives. But, thankfully, everyone around him was determined to make it work and the whole family seemed to want to pull together to make it all run as smoothly as possible. While Sam was no stranger to managing his busy schedule of school, singing practice and whatever else he was doing in his free time, these latest additions were pushing him to the limit and something had to be done.

He was also taking this opportunity to streamline his after-school activities, making sure he wasn't wasting any of his precious time. Over the course of the previous few months, he had begun to focus more clearly on what type of artist he wanted to be, as everything he did needed to lead towards the same end goal. For many years, his ambitions as a singer seemed to be steering him along two very separate paths. As well as his well-documented love of big-voiced, pop divas, he had also fantasised about becoming famous through singing lead roles in musical theatre. His love of musicals may not have matched his love for Whitney, but it came a close second. But recent events had prompted his decision to concentrate fully on becoming a credible pop artist. His main priorities now were acquiring the necessary skills to write more of his own songs and improving his overall performance levels, both on stage and in the recording studio.

First, and with a heavy heart, he decided to quit musical theatre for good. After several very enjoyable years in the chorus of the Bishop's Stortford Youth Theatre, his love of musicals and his ambition to become a West End star hadn't really dwindled at all. In fact, as he felt he'd slightly outgrown the amateur productions closer to home, he asked his parents to find a theatre coach who might help him pursue his stage ambitions further. Eventually the agency he signed with did help him graduate to more professional productions, fulfilling his dream of appearing on stage in London's West End. As part of the junior chorus, Sam performed at several children's showcases and in a particularly memorable production of *South Pacific*. 'It was my first taste of everything, being in a dressing room, having people say, "Well done,"' he told *Rolling Stone*. 'I was really addicted to that feeling.'

But while he'd had a great time, met some life-long friends and gained a lot of confidence simply by being on stage, he eventually began to feel restricted in having to become someone else in order to perform. 'I started to want to be myself on stage,' he told *Self Titled*, 'I found it so much more rewarding to be myself.' No longer content just to sing, he was beginning to blossom into a real artist. His interests had shifted from merely being on stage, following directions and singing other people's songs; he wanted more input and had started to explore his own creativity.

'I lost my love for musicals when I started writing my own songs,' he confessed, before admitting this change of heart had simply come down to priorities as much as anything else. Ultimately, there just wasn't enough time in each day to fit in everything he wanted to do and much as he hated giving it up, he had to make a choice. 'I still love it [musical theatre]. It's just not something I want to do,' he explained. 'Songwriting is too therapeutic for me.' Perhaps it was also his ongoing association with his singing tutor, jazz musician Joanna Eden, during this period which was helping to shape his development as a performer with the need for creative self-expression.

After an extended period away from the limelight, during which time she'd had a baby and started tutoring Sam, Joanna Eden had managed to write and recorded a follow-up to her well-received debut album, *A Little Bird Told Me*. Her sophomore effort, *My Open Eye*, was released independently on her own label, receiving widespread critical acclaim and considerably raising her profile. Soon she was being asked to play alongside some fairly established acts, filling support slots for artists such as Jamie Cullum. Eden often asked Sam to join her onstage as part of her live band, and so her young student provided backing vocals whenever school work and other extracurricular activities permitted.

On one memorable afternoon during the summer of 2007, he joined Eden onstage as she opened for the legendary Buena Vista Social Club at an open-air concert in the grounds of Audley End House, the grand seventeenth-century country house situated only a few miles from Sam's hometown of Great Chishill. Despite near-torrential rain, an eager crowd gathered around the stage early, set up picnics and cheered enthusiastically throughout Eden's set.

While Sam was not taking centre stage during these shows, they provided him with invaluable experience and went a long way towards curing him of any major concerns about performing in front of large crowds. Most of all, he was having fun and doing what he loved: singing. As their relationship had evolved over the years, he had come to count Eden as one of his closest friends and it was perhaps this invaluable exposure to the world of performing on stage as a real musician, a completely different discipline to portraying a character in a play, which was prompting his change of heart.

At last, he was more focused than ever before and things appeared to be moving in the right direction. The dream of being a successful singer-songwriter, releasing an album and performing his own songs in front of an audience of his fans – the end goal he was now working exclusively towards – seemed almost within his reach. But around this time, he began to experience an unexpected crisis of confidence in terms of his physical appearance.

For the first time in his life, he was feeling under pressure to change the way he looked, perhaps feeling self-conscious about the fact he didn't look like most conventional pop stars. 'I used to be really, really big as a child,' he confessed in an interview with *Fader*. 'My weight is something that I have always been very conscious of and sensitive about.' But, however aware he was of being bigger or heavier than the other kids his age, over the years it would seem Sam had accepted it as completely normal and was more or less content with his appearance. He explained to the *Guardian* that it was genetic – his dad's side of the family were skinny, while his mum's side had always been larger – before adding matter-of-factly, 'I take after my mum's side.'

Sam's apparent hunger for success had never really faded despite the many upsets and disappointments he'd endured along the way, but his self-confidence and self-belief had understandably taken a few knocks over the years. He may have been perfectly happy with his weight and his appearance in general, but he was smart enough to know there's always compromise when it comes to achieving any real degree of success in an industry as obsessed with appearance as the music business. With press interviews and photo shoots expected in the near future, it would appear he was being advised he needed to have a particular look, or project a certain image, in order to make the right first impression. And so, probably contrary to his better judgement, he decided it was time for a change and losing weight was the first step in a fairly radical makeover.

Yet again, it was Fred who went that extra mile for his son. While he had been the long-established stay-at-home dad and day-to-day organiser for Sam and his sisters as they were growing up, Fred was now taking direct action to help Sam prepare for the major life changes which were just around the corner. 'My dad basically became a fitness trainer to help me,' Sam revealed. 'He took courses and started to train me, and taught me how to eat better.' Armed with his newly acquired qualifications, Fred began to take control of the entire family's diet and well-being. His aim was not only to help Sam achieve some short-term goals, in terms of his weight and general fitness, he wanted to educate the whole family about nutrition, diet and improve everyone's general health while he was at it.

The new diet and fitness regime was fairly intense and almost certainly must have come as something of a shock to the system for Sam, someone who was a self-confessed over-indulger. Fred introduced a fairly strict exercise routine, even if Sam wasn't always 100 per cent receptive. 'We did loads of running,' he said, 'all the stuff you hate, he tried to make me do.' In terms of diet, he was under strict orders to cut out unnecessary snacks and sugar. Fred was so determined to remove any temptation to cheat he completely banned unhealthy foods from the family shopping list. 'He took out all the fizzy drinks, all the chocolate, all the bad food in the house,' Sam admitted, adding that it wasn't always fair on his two sisters who, unlike him, took after their dad and were naturally thinner. But with Fred's help, he was slowly regaining some of the confidence he had temporarily lost and was feeling ready to face any new challenges coming his way.

So far, 2007 had been a very eventful year for Sam. He'd enjoyed some national exposure from taking part in the *Live and Unsigned* competition process, and while coming second must have been a disappointment, it also served as validation for all the effort he'd put into training his voice. He had made his first tentative steps towards writing his own songs and been lucky enough to spend time recording in a professional studio, but his life was about to get very complicated and the events of the next couple of years would put a huge strain on him and the entire Smith family.

CHAPTER THREE

WALLS COME TUMBLING DOWN

*'I've had such a feminine influence in my life. My mom and
my sisters are very strong women. My best friends are
all girls. I think I've got a bit more woman in me.'*
Sam Smith on acknowledging the female perspectives that
shaped him – *Rolling Stone*

In late 2007, just as Sam's career seemed to be moving in a
wholly satisfying direction, his mum was enjoying a
similarly fulfilling period of professional success. Kate, who
used her maiden name Cassidy at work, had been steadily
rising through the ranks in various banks and financial
trading institutions for the previous twenty years, a career
that proved as challenging as it was financially rewarding.

As a woman in an almost completely male-dominated
profession, she had vowed to work twice as hard as the
majority of her male co-workers, determined to prove she
had the necessary drive to succeed. From very early on in her
career she had been forced to wrestle with difficult decisions
and made countless sacrifices in order to keep her promise.
Now she was beginning to reap the rewards, both in terms of

the professional respect she received from her colleagues and her own personal satisfaction.

Since the mid-1980s Kate had been refining her skills as a financial trader within various positions at Deutsche Bank, NatWest and Citibank, during which time she'd also given birth to her three children. With her husband keen to stay at home and help raise their family, she had managed to avoid taking any prolonged breaks and maintained much of the early momentum she'd created within her career. After the birth of her children, and with no worries about their day-to-day care, she was free to chase promotions whenever and wherever the right position arose. She subsequently moved from one organisation to another every couple of years or so. Before long she was climbing even higher, taking up managerial roles within leading investment brokers, Spear, Leeds & Kellogg and eventually Dutch-based stock traders, Van der Moolen.

Kate was definitely not someone you could ever call complacent. Recognising a distinct shift within her chosen field, she had begun to specialise in the emerging e-commerce side of market trading in the early 2000s and, after joining Dutch state-owned bank ABN AMRO in 2003, had risen to the position of head of technology strategy e-commerce.

She would stay with ABN for the next four years, establishing herself as a highly regarded and integral part of the company's six-person electronic-brokerage team. It was a period of change within the entire financial sector and in the next couple of years following her appointment, the company soon found itself at a crossroads in terms of mapping out its long-term future.

ABN had struggled to maintain the steady growth it had experienced over the previous decade and by 2006 its governing board were calling for drastic action to re-ignite the company's stagnant stock price. Shareholders felt ABN's current share price did not reflect the true value of the company's individual assets and called for the bank to seek acquisition, a merger or for its assets to be broken up and sold off completely. In mid-2007 ABN commenced merger talks with UK's Barclays, but a higher bid from a rival consortium, which included the Royal Bank of Scotland and several European banks, was eventually accepted by a majority of the company's shareholders in early October. The resulting €70bn sale delivered a lucrative €38-a-share offer to its shareholders, but meant uncertainty for ABN's future and left its employees now facing the upheaval of the company's imminent dissolution and the surviving components subsequent integration to their new owners.

Amid this turmoil and undoubtedly fearful of her own job security, Kate decided to jump ship. The *Wall Street Journal* reported at the time that ABN's entire London-based electronic brokerage team had been invited to set up a new division within Tullett Prebon, one of the world's largest inter-dealer money brokers. As a FTSE 250 company, working at the highest level of international finance, Tullett Prebon were responsible for handling financial transactions and brokering private investment deals between companies and banks outside the centralised stock exchange. As the company's newly appointed global head of technology strategy, this was a huge step up for Kate. As part of the team who'd collectively left ABN, she would be spearheading a brand new branch of Tullett Prebon's business, which their chief executive, Terry Smith, described as 'core to the company's growth plans'.

Taking this job was undoubtedly an equally exciting and daunting prospect for Kate. The financial rewards were undeniably substantial, with the *MailOnline* reporting a £200,000 annual salary, a guaranteed annual bonus estimated to be at least £350,000 and the opportunity to earn shares worth as much as a further £350,000 as a performance-related award, but the role itself also came with similarly significant increase in responsibilities and workload.

Back at the Smith family home, it would seem things were ticking along just as before. When Kate received news of her latest promotion, everyone was in the midst of their own mini-dramas, but it was business as usual for Fred who, as always, seemed to have everything completely under control. For quite some time now Sam's dad had been in charge of the day-to-day transport arrangements and he was also the appointment planner and doing a great job at keeping things running smoothly. While Sam was gearing up for his GCSE exams, Lily had now joined her brother at St Mary's and Mabel was just about to make the move from primary to secondary school. Each of these events must have been creating their own small ripples of chaos, but Fred was steering a well-organised and steady ship.

The everyday routines and calm execution of necessary tasks might have been maintained, but it is highly unlikely Kate's change of circumstances had zero effect on the Smith family as a whole. While there were obviously some very welcome financial implications to taking the new job, and the family as a whole undoubtedly benefited from having some extra cash to play around with, the increased responsibilities Kate was now shouldering couldn't have gone unnoticed. It's safe to imagine the growing demands on her time, which went hand-in-hand with her new role, would have meant she spent less free time at home with her family and the pressures of setting up a new business venture must have weighed heavily.

Sam had always been extremely proud of his mum and her achievements, but her recent advancements had been particularly inspiring. Having long admired her strong feminist stance and supported her decision to remain fully focused on her career, he looked back on this time as being incredibly important in his own character development, acknowledging the debt he owed to his mother and her unwavering sense of purpose.

Recalling the dinner parties Kate was so fond of hosting for her work colleagues, Sam told *Fader*, 'I'd watch my mum hold her own until the very end with these men, who were hard businessmen. Just watching her has turned me into someone who really fights for things I believe in, and who has a lot of confidence in what I do.' As Kate became more powerful within her job, Sam has acknowledged the demands on his mother's time meant she was not always at home when he, or his sisters, came home from school. But rather than harbouring feelings of neglect, or resenting his mother's absence, it merely cemented Kate's status as a wholly positive role model for both Sam and his sisters. As well as instilling in him a healthy appreciation of his own early potential, Kate's ambition to succeed and unwavering self-belief had inspired Sam never to give up on his own dreams, but he was all too aware it came at a price. Sam appreciated how hard his mother had worked to get where she was and her continued efforts made him realise that nothing worthwhile came without a fight. While he told *Fader* the set-up at home had undoubtedly given him 'a lot of independence', he admitted his need to prove himself and his determination to stand on his own two feet had sometimes isolated him from others, saying '[it] left me a bit lonely every now and then.'

But in reality, by the start of 2008, it's hard to imagine when Sam would have had a minute to himself, much less the opportunity to actually feel lonely. Around that time, he admitted to *Bent* magazine, 'I love being busy and doing things,' which was just as well because his timetable was now so ridiculously full, it appeared he barely had time to think. While the preliminary recording sessions he'd recently embarked upon were beginning to yield results, for the time being at least, everyone seemed to agree Sam's time was best spent preparing for his upcoming GCSEs.

It must have been hard for him to remain focused on his studies and revise for exams when he was finally catching a glimpse of the life he'd so desperately wanted to be a part of for so long, but if the long list of disappointments he'd been dealt over the last few years had taught him anything, it was to be prepared for every eventuality. Displaying a maturity beyond his years, Sam remained hopeful, if pragmatic about his current situation. 'School grounds me,' he said, 'I also have a strict routine of what to do,' he went on, 'which keeps me from drifting into the clouds.' His highly organised approach to juggling a multitude of tasks was something he'd no doubt picked up from both his parents, but it had been something he'd put in place for himself long before, during his relentless voice training sessions over the previous few years. He stressed, 'I plan most of my evenings so I can get my work done and also have time to do singing practice and things on the musical side.' He added: 'It's hard work, I won't lie, but I cope.'

While all this seems like a lot of extra pressure for anyone on the verge of their sixteenth birthday, Sam felt he'd been working towards this moment for most of his life and he knew the sacrifices he was making would eventually pay off. 'I wouldn't be doing this if I wasn't enjoying myself,' he told *Bent*. 'There's no point. You only live once, and you need to be having fun every minute of every day.' Without question he had inherited something of the incredibly strong work ethic that so evidently drove his mother, but it's just as clear he respected both his parents' opinions and never doubted they only had his best interests at heart.

As Sam had already found out a few years earlier, during the time he'd chosen to 'come out' and be more forthcoming about his sexuality with his close friends and extended family, Fred and Kate provided a very open and supportive home environment and made sure their children were never afraid to share their true feelings on any subject. It seems reasonable to assume they were the ones who were advising Sam to continue his studies and make sure he had qualifications to fall back on.

As a family, the Smiths had already witnessed first-hand some of the more obvious highs and lows associated with

Sam's chosen career, and despite having no discernible background in the entertainment business, they were all too aware it was a precarious profession and he might need protecting from some of its unpredictable pitfalls. While they had no doubts about his talents and had already observed his willingness to work hard and put in the hours to train his voice, everyone around him knew that sometimes it was all down to sheer luck, being in the right place at the right time and the promised 'big break' might inexplicably never happen. The past few years had definitely opened his eyes to some of the more negative aspects of the music industry, but his dedication never seemed to waver. Rather than emerging disillusioned or jaded, he saw everything thrown at him, good or bad, as a learning curve and stored it away for future reference.

It was with this mindset that he approached the run-up to his GCSEs and his determination paid dividends when the time came to get the results. Momentarily focusing more closely on his schoolwork and exam preparation was not something Sam saw as a distraction from his main goal; he regarded it all as part of the same plan. 'I made sure I got very good grades at GCSE so I will always be able to return to education,' he told *Bent*. 'All I want to do is sing, and school or no school, I will do that. I want to follow my dreams, and having the grades to fall back on is just an extra added bonus.'

He had never been closer to realising his dream of becoming a professional singer, but thankfully he seemed to be grasping the reality of his situation and refused to be swept up in the 'fantasy'. Recent entanglements with bad managers, and the promised deals which failed to materialise, had made him much more level-headed and businesslike about his future and having a solid education and qualifications now seemed just as important as everything he'd been doing to train his voice.

With his GCSEs behind him, he had a window of opportunity to more or less concentrate full-time on recording, hoping to complete the songs he'd been working on in his spare time. He was still at the earliest stages of realising his potential as a songwriter and while all the songs he had been working on so far were ones he'd had a hand in choosing, they were all written by other people.

Recently, he had signed a deal with Venus & Mars Music (V&M), a small west London-based independent label, and had been working with a team of fairly seasoned writers and musicians. Among them were Victoria Hemmings (who recorded under the name Ziggi Baker), William John 'Bob' Pearce and John Conlon, a songwriting team who'd previously worked under the name SupaSub and had a long-standing working relationship with V&M Music. All three had spent the last twenty years trying to attract the attention of the major record companies, chasing deals but never being quite lucky enough to have all the pieces fall into place at the same time. They had performed together as Land, Lovatux and eventually Independence, coming frustratingly close to breaking through after signing with Mercury Records in 1994 and East/West a few years later. Both deals had ended badly, either through record company bosses' reevaluation or due to the music industry's general lack of stability.

As Hemmings would state on the team's *Walking to a*

Different Beat website, 'We were literally spat out because of circumstances that had nothing to do with us and a lot to do with a faltering music industry.' Then, as now, most high-profile labels seemed to operate a frustrating revolving door policy which often saw key personnel move from label to label, with the artists they signed left behind at the mercy of their successors. After one too many disappointments at the hands of the mainstream music industry, Hemmings, Pearce and Conlon decided to sign a deal with Keystone Records, a label set up by Hemmings' management team, and to concentrate on songwriting for themselves and the label's fledgling roster of acts.

Thus, the one-stop-shop of Venus & Mars Music and Keystone Records seemed to be able to offer aspiring artists the opportunity to work with some experienced musicians and writers, and as an outlet for any subsequent recordings. As part of this set-up, the team's songwriting skills were naturally being used, and some of the songs they created then would surface several times over the next few years, either as part of Lovatux's repertoire, for their individual solo projects or recorded by the label's other signings. So, despite the partnership having been all but dissolved by the time Sam Smith was signed to Venus & Mars, their songs were some of the first he was given to record.

The first of Sam's recordings to see the light of day would be 'Bad Day All Week', a song which had appeared on Lovatux's unreleased, self-titled album and then latterly as the B-side to their 1996 single, 'Something'. To say 'Bad Day All Week' sounds nothing like the Sam Smith we now know is something of an understatement. Built around a driving guitar riff and a relentless drumbeat, it has more in common with Lenny Kravitz or Terence Trent D'Arby than Whitney Houston or Mariah Carey. But, despite a complete lack of subtlety, the very beginnings of Sam's trademark wide vocal range, and in particular his falsetto, can be heard trying to shine through the rather light production.

Ahead of its scheduled release as a single, the decision was made to try and broaden the reach of 'Bad Day All Week' with a series of dance and club mixes. At the start of August 2008, the UK singles chart reflected the on-going interest in a wide variety of urban and dance music. From Dizzee Rascal and Calvin Harris's cutting-edge mash-up of UK hip hop and electronic dance music (EDM) on 'Dance Wiv Me' and several more straightforward R&B hits from the likes of Busta Rhymes, Flo Rida and Rihanna to cheesy Euro-dance tracks courtesy of Basshunter and Cascada, there was a vibrant and diverse market to tap into. The extensive remix package for 'Bad Day All Week' reflected that diversity, with hopes that the song would receive significant airplay, in one form or another, from as wide a range of radio stations as possible.

Aside from the standard 'radio' version of the track, there were several 'club-friendly' reworkings by established DJs and remixers. These included long-time Boy George collaborator Kinky Roland and Swedish producer Per QX. Unfortunately, even at the time of release, these remixes of 'Bad Day All Week' sounded a little dated compared to the super-slick productions of the fast-emerging EDM artists, best exemplified by the likes of Calvin Harris, Avicii and Swedish House Mafia, and the song failed to make much of an impact outside some fairly specialist club charts.

It was a good sign that someone had enough faith in the project to commission a promo video to promote the song's release, but it's fairly obvious from the end result that good intentions alone are not enough. Although the promo has long since disappeared from the Internet, it's clear from several published stills that it's not Michael Jackson's 'Thriller'. It features Sam, in full school uniform, lip-syncing to the song as he walks around the streets of a suburban town. *Sugarscape*, the entertainment and fashion website aimed at teenage girls, described it as 'hilarious', before adding sarcastically, 'We're not quite sure which bit is our favourite – the fact that [Sam] keeps bumping into every single person he walks past, or the terrible, TERRIBLE acting skills of the extras.'

It was clear he wasn't going to be picking up any trophies at the MTV Video Music Awards that year, but at least he now had his own music video. While the video might have missed the mark, a second wave of more generic dance remixes did start to gain some traction on a couple of UK and international club charts and he was beginning to get calls from press and media interested in running features and interviews.

Convinced that 'the Singing Schoolboy' angle would appeal to a wide range of media outlets, and buoyed by some positive feedback for 'Bad Day All Week', Sam continued work on his work at a steady pace. More songs from SupaSub were dusted down and given to him, among them tracks previously recorded by Lovatux, Bob Pearce as a solo artist and another of Venus & Mars' acts, Lindsey Butler. These included 'A Little Melancholy', 'Show A Little Mercy' and the song that would eventually become the album's title track, 'Time Won't Wait'. Ranging from Prince-inspired, funky slow-jams and electro-pop anthems to heartfelt piano ballads, the album certainly attempts to showcase Sam's exceptional vocal range. Perhaps strongest of all is 'Momentarily Mine', a ballad co-written by Lindsey Butler, which sounds vaguely similar to Terence Trent D'Arby's 'Sign Your Name' and hints at the type of confessional lyrics Sam would later explore to much greater success on the songs from his *In the Lonely Hour* album.

By the end of the summer, he had already returned to St Mary's. While he continued his studies there, he completed the recordings earmarked for his first album, as well as fulfilling press and media requests for features and interviews, which had started to surface in the wake of 'Bad Day All Week'. Sam was finding it tough – he had some big decisions to make about which subjects to choose for his A-level studies – but he was typically upbeat about the multitude of exciting new experiences. 'There are frustrating factors to school life,' he told *Bent*, 'but I always have recording sessions to look forward to.' He went on to say, 'I'm loving it. I loved the recording period so much, but the photo shoots are also so much fun because you never know what the result will be. I like that excitement, and I love fashion and that allows me to express myself.'

Sam was fully embracing his new lifestyle and making sure he was right at the centre of everything that was unfolding around him. But just as things seemed to be coming together, his mother was about to deliver news that would turn the whole Smith family's world upside down and bring his dream crashing down around him.

As reported on the *MailOnline* website, in September 2008 Kate was called into a meeting with her boss, Paul Humphrey, and Tullett Prebon's head of human resources, Mark Scally. Humphrey and Kate's career paths had been in-synch since they'd both worked at Spear, Leeds & Kellogg back in 1999, and they had subsequently moved to the same companies, at the same time, ever since.

So it must have come as quite a shock when, without warning, she was summarily dismissed on the spot. With less than a year gone on the three-year contract she'd signed back in 2007, it was a major rug-pull for Kate and one she must have initially struggled to comprehend.

It can't have been a comfortable trip back to Great Chishill on that particular afternoon but at least she knew she would have Fred and her family's support while she tried to make sense of it all. She was adamant she had been given only positive feedback regarding her performance at work prior to her dismissal and she was keen to receive more details of the reason for it. Eventually, she found out that Tullett Prebon had accused her of hiring a friend to work at the firm and of misusing the company's time and resources in order to promote Sam and further his music career. Kate decided to challenge her dismissal in court. It was obviously going to be a long, drawn-out process and the whole family would need to rally round her in order to get through it.

While there was obviously a lot to be angry and upset about surrounding the whole unfortunate situation, Sam felt particularly aggrieved about the fact that he, and his dream of having a singing career, were somehow being used as ammunition against his own mother. 'I think she was just very proud that her son could sing,' Sam told *Fader*. 'She wasn't a pushy parent. It was actually my dad that used to push me.' Elaborating in an interview with the *Guardian*, he insisted, 'My dad, bless him, is the one who should get credit for that,' and explained that although she'd always been supportive about his desire to become a singer, his mother never had the time or aspirations to micro-manage his career – not forgetting that there was also a long list of former managers who could probably attest to that fact. Meanwhile, in the *Telegraph*, Sam tried to make light of the situation by joking, 'My poor dad's driving me around London for years and then my mum gets all the credit,' but in reality the case would have a serious and far-reaching effect on the entire family.

Kate decided to launch a damages claim against Tullett Prebon, with the local *Herts & Essex Observer* reporting: 'She wants £410,643.83 in lost salary, £900,000 in missed guaranteed bonuses for 2008–10 plus a sum of shares she missed out on worth an estimated £350,000 as well as a "sum in respect of the value of remaining benefits" plus "such other further relief as the court shall see fit".' With such large sums at stake, it's hardly surprising the story was picked up by the national press and tabloids but, clearly, it wasn't exactly the type of media attention Sam was looking for at this stage in his career.

When the story started to break at the beginning of February 2009, Sam had already released another single from the initial batch of songs recorded at Venus & Mars. 'When It's Alright' was another Hemmings, Conlon and Pearce composition, and while it was a summery, pop-soul track in its original form,

'When It's Alright' had received the same remix treatment as 'Bad Day All Week'. 'When It's Alright' was serviced to club DJs in new mixes by Kinky Roland and Per Qx, the same remixers who had re-worked Sam's previous release. But it was new mixes by Danish producer Benjamin Pedersen, using his DJ name 'Kid Massive', which attracted greater attention. Pedersen's remix transformed the song into a credible, deep-house club track, with an irresistibly catchy chorus hook and a mid-point breakdown which stripped the track back, leaving a stunning a cappella vocal passage, showcasing Sam's voice to extraordinary effect.

While the song hadn't quite broken into the mainstream, 'When It's Alright' seemed to be creating the desired buzz and was attracting coverage from several of the more 'serious' dance music sites and publications. It was being talked about in far more credible terms, gaining positive reviews. Perhaps most importantly of all, Sam, and in particular his voice, was undoubtedly more of a focal point than ever before. But this in itself raised some unavoidable problems: the voice on the recording didn't really match the image of the sixteen-year-old boy in the promotional photographs. Sam's image was nowhere near as sophisticated as the sound of his voice and it's unlikely any of the trendy clubbers dancing to his song at Ministry of Sound (or in clubs up and down the country) were picturing the singer wearing a school uniform. No matter how good he sounded on the recording, there was a huge divide between Sam and what was generally expected of artists working in the dance music genre.

Even so, though, 'When It's Alright' continued to create a buzz through the first few months of 2009 and international interest in the track was growing. Eventually, Munich-based dance label, Kosmo Records, approached V&M Music and signed a worldwide license deal for the track, as well as taking an option to remix the whole of Sam's album for other territories when it was eventually released. 'When It's Alright' was immediately re-promoted with new mixes by German DJ and producer Tom Novy.

Over the years, Kosmo had made a name for themselves as one of the most exciting and innovative underground dance labels in Europe. They had nurtured several of the genre's biggest stars and crossed over into the mainstream in 2002 with Tomcraft's 'Loneliness', which reached No. 1 on the UK singles chart a year later when it was licensed to Ministry of Sound's off-shoot label, Data Records. Novy was one of Kosmo's most established signings, having made a name for himself as an in-demand DJ and remixer, as well as being a successful recording artist in his own right.

Accompanied by artwork and promotional material that did not feature any images of Sam, 'When It's Alright' was given another push in the UK. Promotional CD copies of the single concentrated on the impressive credentials of the talent involved in putting the remix package together and boasted, 'This looks set to blow!' The track made a strong showing in the specialist pop/dance charts, but for Sam the growing popularity of his song and the exposure he was getting across Europe had very little impact on his day-to-day life. Work continued on completing the album, with some of his earliest recordings revisited, and sections of songs re-recorded, as his confidence in the studio grew. Plans for the album's release were firming up and Venus &

Mars' website confidently stated his debut, *Time Won't Wait*, would be launched soon.

All this was playing out against the backdrop of Kate's damages claim and by the end of April 2009 a date had been set for her case against Tullett Prebon to be heard in the High Court. Expected to last for four days, the court case was due to begin on 2 November. The looming legal proceedings threw the entire family into a state of limbo, with Kate effectively unemployed and unable to look for a new job until after the trial.

Obviously it must have been a worrying time for everyone, and while they were hardly destitute and homeless, the Smiths faced a long period of turmoil and financial uncertainty. Sam had been lucky enough to benefit from his mother's success, and while he has stated their financial situation made them comfortable – they had travelled, and Sam has recalled annual Christmas shopping trips to London and visits to Harrods – it wasn't something they took for granted. Perhaps, as Sam pointed out in the *Daily Mail*, this was due to the family's rapid rise to a relatively wealthy lifestyle, but as Kate's employment ended suddenly he noted, 'Just as quick was the decline,' adding, 'We were in a whole different situation.'

As with the vast majority of legal disputes of this type, the matter was eventually settled by agreement between the parties. The outcome of Kate's case was not published nor released to the public and the finer details of the agreement she reached with her former employers remained a private matter. The *Daily Star Sunday* noted, 'It is not clear if her case and settlement was awarded by a judge or if Tullett Prebon made an out-of-court settlement,' before suggesting she had received a '£800,000 payout', a figure later repeated in a separate piece in the *Daily Mail*.

The end of the court case brought some degree of closure for Kate, but as 2009 ended, it was clear the full weight of everything that had happened was still exerting an enormous amount of pressure on the Smith family. On top of all the uncertainty surrounding Kate's future employment, Sam's career seemed to have slipped backwards into another frustrating period of inertia: 2009 had come and gone, and his debut album still hadn't been given a proper release.

Realistically, there was no real momentum behind the project without a hit single or some solid airplay to highlight the album even existed. With nothing driving people towards the album, it would have struggled to achieve any initial impact and sales would have been virtually non-existent. Two singles had been released, but had failed to find much of an audience in their original form. The Official Chart Company website shows sales of less than 300 copies for 'Bad Day All Week' and although the various remixes of 'When It's Alright' had received widespread praise, and achieved decent exposure abroad, the actual single had experienced similarly sluggish sales in the UK.

What interest there was in Sam at this point was being generated by some credible but relatively niche club remixes and, in real terms, no one had any idea it was his voice on the record. Inevitably, this must have given the team at V&M doubts about where to position him as an artist and prompted a re-think as to which direction his musical output should take. If the album's mix of pop, rock and piano ballads was not showing him in the best light, perhaps a more dance-orientated, club sound would be a better fit. For Sam, the more pop-orientated tracks on the album were undoubtedly enough of a departure from the type of music he'd been dreaming about creating for almost a decade and he had little interest in becoming predominately a dance act.

No doubt, he was all too aware that at this stage in his career a certain degree of compromise was needed, but he must have worried he was drifting further and further away from the genres of music he loved and the type of songs being recorded by the artists he idolised. Sam's overriding passion was for soul music and his dream was to sing powerful ballads and the type of uptempo pop/soul numbers Whitney Houston had made her own in the 1980s and 1990s, all of which seemed a long way from the tracks he had so far completed as part of the *Time Won't Wait* project. As he approached his eighteenth birthday, it was clear some changes needed to be made in terms of his music career and it appears the time had come to press the reset button.

CHAPTER FOUR

MOVING MOUNTAINS

'Deep down in me there was never a question... From day one
I had a quiet confidence that everything would be OK.'
Sam Smith on keeping the faith - *Guardian*, August 2014

2009 had been a fairly momentous year for everyone at 'The Pink House' and while much of what happened through-out the course of the previous twelve months was deemed best forgotten by Sam and the rest of his family, some invaluable lessons had also been learnt. Moving forward into 2010, it would seem his number one priority was getting his music career back on track. Unhappy with the way the *Time Won't Wait* project had turned out and unsure if the album was ever going to get a release, he faced continued frustration surrounding his label's debate about which market they felt he should be targeting. Having achieved a certain degree of success with a more dance-orientated sound, perhaps the thinking was to remix the songs on the album and focus on altering his image accordingly.

Whatever the final reason, Sam decided to end his

association with V&M Music and walk away from the deal. It would seem he had considered his options carefully and although it must have been a difficult choice to make, he was determined to remain positive about the whole situation. This latest venture had brought him closer than ever to achieving his dream. He'd been able to catch a glimpse behind the closed curtain of the music industry and gained some valuable professional experiences along the way; he'd been rubbing shoulders with accomplished musicians, songwriters and music business insiders and witnessed the inner workings of a recording studio for the first time. 'It was good and bad,' he told the *Guardian*. 'The good was that my recording ability, now, has benefited. The bad was that there were a lot of false promises.'

Ironically, despite ending his deal with V&M Music, the songs Sam recorded during this time would come back to haunt him at a later stage. As the deal Kosmo Records made with V&M gave them the right to remix any of the tracks from his unreleased album, it's almost inevitable that some of those tracks would surface once his *In the Lonely Hour* album was released and Sam Smith became a marketable name. Thus, in 2013, 'When It's Alright', now completely transformed and credited to Juun featuring Sam Smith, was re-released and became a small club hit in Germany and across much of Europe. The following year, 'Momentarily Mine' – the piano ballad from Sam's V&M record – emerged, now simply titled 'Moments', under the name Freddy Verano featuring Sam Smith. Radically transformed, this song had a similarly widespread release and inspired Kosmo to re-examine the entire *Time Won't Wait* project. Ultimately they would commission remixes for every track on the album and re-name the collection, *Sam Smith: The Lost Tapes*, with a planned release in mid-2015.

It's easy to speculate that much of Sam's desire to win back control over his own career was inspired by the situation his mother now found herself in. Kate may have had over twenty years' experience in her field, but she was in her mid-forties. In fact, the fall-out from the court case had been something of reality check for the whole family. While money was obviously now an issue in a way it hadn't been for a while, the real wake-up call was how certain sections of Kate and Fred's social circle reacted to the family's new circumstances. People they'd previously thought of as close friends were suddenly not so close after all and it forced everyone to be more suspicious about those they chose to let into their tight-knit circle. As the oldest child, and arguably the most sensitive member of the household, it seems Sam in particular took much of the subsequent disruption to heart and had the most obvious negative reaction to everything that was going on around him. He had undoubtedly started to feel a growing sense of powerlessness about his future. Dealing with the outcome of Kate's dismissal – the previously unimaginable precariousness of his family's financial situation and the strain it must have put on his parents' relationship – was hard enough, but combined with the growing dissatisfaction he felt surrounding the direction his music career was taking, it was just too much for him to process.

Sam was a naturally hard-working and organised person. He'd spent years making sure he stayed on top of schoolwork and exams while squeezing in his extracurricular music activities – the singing lessons, gigs and, eventually, recording sessions – as well as holding down a part-time job in a local shop, taking part in sports and maintaining a healthy social life. But it seems his immediate reaction to the relative chaos he was experiencing at this time was to try and grab back some degree of control.

With this in mind, he began to rebel a little. Soon he was clashing with the authority figures in his life, acting up and misbehaving in a way he had never done before. There was no denying he was mature for his age. He had, for much of his childhood and early teens, shown uncommon single-mindedness and self-discipline in terms of organising his own after-school timetable, but suddenly he seemed to want to party more, drink with his friends and, for someone with the reputation of being a 'good boy' at school, he was exhibiting some decidedly 'bad boy' tendencies. 'I was making up for lost time a little bit,' he told *Fader*. 'I went a bit mental. I remember my friends all wanted to go to bars and I just wanted to be a street rat and sit on the streets and drink because I never got to do that.'

In another interview with *Rolling Stone*, he recalled an incident when he'd lied to his parents and teachers, skipped classes and headed off to London to get to the front of the queue for Lady Gaga's 'Monsters Ball' show at the O2 Arena. In order to get to the venue early enough and secure a place near the stage, he had forged a note from his parents asking his teachers to excuse him from school for the day. While the letter worked and Sam admitted, 'I was front row, fully Gaga'd up!' his plan was far from foolproof. He left the fake note open on a school computer and when it was discovered, he was forced to face the consequences. He was given three days' detention, as well as being punished at home. Looking back, he obviously feels it was well worth the sacrifice, saying, 'I'd do it again in a heartbeat,' but at the time it was fairly out of character and symptomatic of deeper issues surrounding the uncertainty and turmoil in his life.

As well as the direct impact on Sam's behaviour back then, he seems to have carried some of the wariness he developed during this time forward into adult life. 'It made me a very paranoid person,' he told the *Guardian*, 'Even now I get paranoid if one of my team doesn't reply or seems angry with me – I'm like, oh no, that's it.' But as he would later tell the *Telegraph*, he took some positives away from his mum's dismissal. 'There's a fire in me,' he stressed, 'there's a fire that ignited in me on the day that happened.' Having watched Kate struggle to balance her home and work life throughout most of his childhood, to him she seemed indestructible. Sam had definitely never thought of his mum as vulnerable and discovering that even the strongest person he knew had a breaking point, along with the perceived injustice she'd suffered, was a tough pill to swallow. He would tell the *London Evening Standard*, 'what it did was really give me the hunger to look after her. She deserves the world and that's what I'm trying to do, give it to her.'

It was with this increased sense of determination, and with a renewed hunger to succeed, that he entered his final year at school. With a decent set of GCSE results already in the bag, he had been working towards achieving similar results with his A-levels. But it's safe to say, unlike most of his classmates, who were aiming for specific grades to secure their preferred college or university places, Sam still considered these formal qualifications as something to fall back on and they'd only ever be necessary if he was forced to put his 'Plan B' into action. He told *Pigeons and Planes*, 'I remember sitting with my career advisor and she was like, "Right, so what are you doing? Have you figured out what you're doing?" And my answer was literally, "I'm going to move to London and be a well-known singer." That was it.' While Sam had every confidence he knew what he was doing, his teacher was obviously not so sure – 'You could see she was just like, "What the f*ck are you doing, you're crazy."'

Thankfully, his parents had never lost their faith in their son. It's clear they had been right beside him during the many ups and downs he'd experienced over the previous decade or so – and they had obviously been through a few tribulations of their own – but Sam admits, 'My parents never doubted me. Not once.' The united front shown by his parents, in terms of encouraging him and his sisters to pursue their individual dreams, was a much-needed constant during this period of massive disruption.

It's fairly ironic then that, while Fred and Kate's stability as parents remained firm, their marriage had effectively started to fall apart. In the wake of the traumatic events of the previous twelve months, the whole family had decided to take a week's holiday together in New York City. It was around the time of Sam's eighteenth birthday and undoubtedly everyone was glad to finally have something to celebrate. Shortly after arriving, clearly excited to make the most of their time, they decided to 'do the tourist thing' and spend their first day exploring the city and taking in a few of the most popular sights. It was undoubtedly a huge relief for Sam and his sisters to get away from everything back home. It's easy to forget that both Lily and Mabel were still in their early teens. They too had been forced to shoulder extra responsibilities at home and the events of the previous year had taken them on as much of an emotional rollercoaster as Sam. This trip was the perfect opportunity for everyone to depressurise and work through some of the difficulties that had started to dominate their lives back in the UK.

Within this welcome and carefree atmosphere, it came as quite a surprise when, just as they were walking underneath the Brooklyn Bridge, Sam was suddenly aware that one of his sisters had started crying. He later explained to *Rolling Stone* that one of his sisters had accidentally seen their dad sending a text to another woman and had realised what was going on. 'We had no choice but to go for walks through Central Park and talk about it,' he stated. 'My sisters would cry. I would cry. We all dealt with it suddenly.' Admittedly, the unwelcome news that his parents were in the process of splitting up and had, in fact, already decided to divorce came out of the blue and hit Sam and his siblings pretty hard.

But he now recognises the positives in their situation; he believes their relationship as a family was ultimately strengthened by the fairly unusual circumstances in which they all found out and the actual divorce process his parents went through was relatively painless. 'It was actually the best holiday we've ever had in our lives,' Sam explained to *Pigeons and Planes*, 'because we were all stuck in New York together for the whole week and had to kind of get on with it as a family.' With no escape, they had been immediately forced to deal with all the emotional fall-out and Sam remains convinced it only served to reinforce their already-solid family bond. 'It's the reason why we're all so close now. It's mad, isn't it? My parents had, like, the nicest breakup you could think of and they're best friends now.'

On returning to Great Chishill, the whole family was now thrown into a state of flux. For Sam it must have seemed like the perfect moment to make the break from his old life and strike out on his own. After a brief period where he found himself commuting from Cambridgeshire into London every day to work in a bar in the St Paul's area of the city, he decided he needed to actually move out of the family home and get a place of his own. As usual, Fred and Kate were incredibly supportive and fully backed his decision, helping and advising in whatever way they could. 'Thank God,' Sam told BBC News, 'My mum and dad had faith in me.'

So it was, with his parents' full blessing, that Sam decided to move to London as soon as he was finished with school. While many of his friends were contemplating gap years, taking time out to travel or moving away from home to begin their studies, Sam was planning to make one final push at setting himself up as a professional singer and hoped to finally launch a career in music on his own terms. It seems this decision, at least in part, was inspired by reading press reports about Lady Gaga's own struggles to make it as a singer. He told *Fader*, 'I remember when Lady Gaga was coming out, watching her and hearing her story of how she hustled in New York for everything. I remember thinking,

"Right, that's what I need to do."' It's unclear how much actual 'hustling' Sam had to do, but his mind was made up.

Sam remains adamant the move was something he masterminded and funded himself. He never took for granted the freedom and support his parents had given him through his teenage years but he was equally eager to dispel the prevailing myth that he was merely the product of a typically pushy 'stage family'. He insisted to *Fader*, 'This is my work. This is me moving to London, and me singing and honing my craft. This is my choice. This is my passion and my drive.' Thus, it has been reported he ended up renting a room in an east London flat owned by his then manager. His latest adventure was soon underway.

Sam would later describe those first few months in London as something of a reality check. He told *Self Titled*, 'I had probably three or four friends in London, which was tough,' and while he was never really alone for long periods of time, he began to understand that loneliness was something that often went hand in hand with independence. Thankfully, among the few people he did know in London were a couple of girls, Tiffany Clare and Beth Rowe, who he knew from back home and counted as two of his closest friends. Sam says he's been friends with Tiffany and Beth since he was about four years old, meeting them shortly after his family first moved to Great Chishill. Beth had been Sam's 'partner-in-crime' during much of his time at the Bishop's Stortford musical theatre group, and he and Tiffany had become 'soul-mates' over the years. Sam would often refer to Tiffany as 'my wife' on Twitter, before adding, 'Such a couple... without the sexy time.'

After spending time in the Limehouse area of east London, Sam would end up moving south of the Thames and began sharing a flat with Tiffany in the Stockwell area. Beth would eventually join them as their new flatmate in August 2012 and they quickly settled into a routine of Sunday lunches ('Sunday Munch', as they called it), long nights in front of the TV binge-watching *Lost* and *Cougar Town* and the odd midnight gym session.

Obviously taking up most of Sam's time was his full-time bar job. It had become very clear, very quickly, that if he wanted to stand on his own two feet, he had to make enough money to pay his rent, cover the bills and buy food. But outside the long and arduous work hours, he was trying to live life to the full and the rest of his free time was soon swallowed up absorbing everything London had to offer. Like most youngsters living away from home for the first time, enjoying a newfound sense of freedom and self-sufficiency, Sam felt an overriding desire to party hard and grab every opportunity to let his hair down.

In many respects, aside from a brief spell of rebellion a year or so earlier, he had led a fairly sheltered life growing up in Great Chishill. Even before his teenage years, he'd spent the majority of his free time concentrating on training his voice and improving his singing. 'I was doing shows every day, or I'd be doing rehearsals for shows,' Sam told *Fader*. 'Every single day after school I'd go to rehearsals and sleep. I remember the first time I drank was at an after-school party when I was sixteen.' He also admitted that despite having 'come out' at a relatively early age, and feeling completely comfortable with his own sexuality, his experience of mixing with other gay men was limited. 'To the age of sixteen, I'd never met another gay person,' he confessed to the *London Evening Standard*. 'When I moved to London, the gay scene was a real eye-opener. Some things were amazing, but other things are very dark.'

Sam described a 'queer bashing' incident, which happened shortly after he arrived in London, when some other guys took exception to him. 'I got punched in the neck in the street,' he revealed. 'I used to wear a bit of make-up. I had pink earphones on and was talking really loud. It was definitely a homophobic attack.' He has admitted this was no easy time in his life, with several periods of feeling relatively lonely and unhappy. He told *Rolling Stone*, 'I had a lot of one-night stands. I met a few dodgy friends, people I'm definitely not friends with now.'

But it wasn't in his nature to be consumed by the negative aspects of his newfound independence and he never lost sight of his main motivation for leaving home. Primarily, he was in London to be closer to the music industry. He felt this was the best place to build the network of contacts and collaborators necessary to help him move a little bit closer to fully realising his dream. He'd hoped to meet like-minded musicians, singers and songwriters who could offer the type of support and guidance he needed to finally get his foot in the door. In reality, making those connections and finding a way in was proving to be a little more elusive. He was finding it hard to get anyone to listen to his music and there was no one rushing to offer him a record contract at this stage either.

But he was realistic enough to grasp what was fact and what was fantasy. He'd quickly realised no one was going to hand him his dream on a plate and the streets of London were definitely not paved with gold. Sam knew the type of success he craved would only come as a result of hard work and he expected to have to make a few sacrifices along the way. Already he'd put in a great deal of effort to get this far and he had faced more than his fair share of disappointments in the past, so it was clear his eyes were wide open in terms of understanding what needed to be done.

Ultimately, if there was anything he'd inherited from his mum, it was a fiercely ambitious streak and the determination to beat the odds if things looked like they were stacked against you. Sam quickly realised for something good to come out of the situation he was now in, he had to make it happen for himself. So, with his resolve intact, he continued to chip away at whatever barrier he felt was keeping him tantalisingly just out of reach of his dream, frustratingly rooted on the wrong side of the VIP rope, convinced his big break was just around the corner.

For over a year he kept the faith, but eventually long hours at the bar and the endless monotony started to wear him down. He told *Pigeons and Planes*, 'I really hustled and grinded.' He confessed to BBC News, 'I used to work in a toilet in a bar. I didn't have to talk to anyone, I just had to clean up everything that happened at night – which was horrendous.' Even as he moved from one bar to another, taking more of a responsible role and supposedly dealing with a better class of customer, he knew his heart wasn't really in it. 'The bar I worked in last, which I helped to manage, was in the City, so there was a lot of chucking drunk people out,' he said. '[It could] get a bit lairy,' before stating he would turn 'a bit Peggy Mitchell' in order to deal with potential troublemakers. This definitely wasn't where he wanted to be and he was spending less and less time actually singing. 'I was working full-time, so I didn't really have time,' he told *Self Titled*. 'On my downtime, I'd write, and try and meet people and write with them.'

It became clear his job was taking up so much of his time that he was barely finding time to sing at all and he began to feel he was actually neglecting his voice. 'There was a moment where I said, "I'm gonna give this just one more year and then I'm done. Because I just can't do it anymore. I can't clean toilets while I watch my friends live their lives." I wasn't growing as a human being; I felt like I was stuck in that job and not enjoying my life.'

While Sam never really lost faith that his voice was something special, which undoubtedly set him apart from the majority of other singers he met, he was beginning to worry about the future. From early childhood, as soon as he discovered he had a voice, Sam only really had one driving ambition – to earn a living as a professional singer and hopefully make enough money to provide a better life for himself and his family – but for the first time in his life he had begun speculating about what he'd do if it just never happened. 'I was basically saying, I give myself one more year to do this, then I give up,' he told the *Guardian*. 'If it doesn't happen next year I'm going to leave and travel and see the world.' He went on to outline his long-term goal: 'I would have opened up a flower shop in Italy,' and explained, 'I used to love going to the garden centre as a kid. It made me feel relaxed. It would have just been a calm, beautiful life.'

Thankfully, the florist business's loss was the music industry's gain and it never quite came to be, but it was obvious Sam was beginning to lose confidence. It seems his crisis of faith had less to do with belief in his own voice – that remained wholly intact – but more in terms of who he might have to become, and the image he was expected to project, in order to fit in with the music industry's ideas of what was fashionable and marketable. 'I was at the point where I was going, "I will do anything",' he told the *Telegraph*. 'I was saying, "You can clone me into whatever you want. I just want to be a singer. I don't want to be working in this bar any more. I will do whatever you tell me to do".' Later, he told *Teen Vogue*, 'I wanted this so badly that I was willing to completely sell myself to become a pop star because I was poor. No one was complimenting me anymore, so I started to lose faith. I thought, I'm going to have to dress a certain way, lose weight, or sing a certain type of song.'

For Sam, this chapter in his life was to become a real turning point. There's little doubt, even at this stage in his career, that he possessed a rare talent and the necessary conviction to succeed, but getting that first big break was proving to be harder than he'd hoped. While the faith he'd always had in his own potential remained steadfastly intact, he was slowly beginning to realise self-belief alone was not going to be enough. He was downhearted, but not defeated. Thanks to his mother's influence, he had developed an independent streak, which had served him well so far. He'd grown up wilful, determined and, at times, stubborn, but at this point he was the first to admit he really needed help. He had put his trust in others before and it hadn't always worked out the way he wanted, but this time Sam was a little older and much more in control of his own life. He was considerably better prepared for the ups and downs a career in the music industry could throw at him and he felt ready to make the necessary compromises.

Sam was confident his past experiences had taught him to be suitably cautious. He was looking for someone who not only saw his potential as an artist and had similar faith in his talent, he wanted someone who shared his love of music and understood his motivations for becoming a singer. While this might seem like a fairly tall order considering the difficulty he was experiencing in getting anyone to sit up and take notice, it turns out he had already met the man who fitted that description perfectly – he just didn't realise it. Thankfully, their paths were about to cross once again, and this time their reunion would have a seismic impact on the rest of Sam's life and career.

CHAPTER FIVE

SETTING SAIL

'We got so close to the fame and the lights/
Watching the stars tonight/Little Sailor, let's sail tonight.'
Sam Smith – 'Little Sailor'

J ust as Sam's confidence seemed to be at an all-time low, and his resolve began to waver slightly, he wrote and recorded a song called 'Little Sailor'. Although it has never been officially released, and it's unlikely his fans are ever going to hear him perform the song live at any point, 'Little Sailor' is arguably the most important song he has ever written. While two separate profiles of Sam's career in the *Guardian* recently branded the song as 'self-pitying' and 'juvenilia', it is in fact something altogether more bold and significant, something Sam himself would later acknowledge when he affectionately nicknamed his new army of fans as his 'Little Sailors'.

Aside from offering a precise summation of his state of mind at that exact moment, the song's lyrics neatly expressed much of the underlying tenacity that had been key to Sam's survival up to that point. It also confirmed he understood he wasn't going to get everything he wanted without a fight and there was still plenty of work to be done. The song described someone who had come tantalisingly close to realising their dream of finding 'the fame and the lights', but had been left disappointed, asking if the music industry was in fact going to 'take the best of me' and 'swallow all of me'. 'Among the lyrics was the couplet, 'Six different managers all filled with good intent/Promised me the world but I haven't seen anything yet.'

Sam revealed in an interview with *Fader*: 'It was a song to myself to say, "Hold out for one more year, and if you're still being let down and you're still being promised the world and nothing's happening, life's too short. Go and travel and be a twenty-year-old-boy".' Elsewhere in the lyrics, Sam describes his eagerness to do whatever it takes to find acceptance ('Willing to do anything if I write a hit song/And I'll ride this tide/I'll put some makeup on/And I'll shock the crowd') and ends with a declaration of gratitude towards his parents for their unequivocal support. All things considered, it seemed 'Little Sailor' had little to do with Sam looking for sympathy or feeling sorry for himself; instead it appeared to act as some kind of status report and mission statement all rolled into one. It was this 'declaration of intent' which would prove to be his most valuable calling card when, around the time of his nineteenth birthday, he found himself 'between managers' for the sixth time.

While the thought of starting all over again and launching the search for No.7 wasn't something he relished, he had been there before. Toughened by his previous experiences, he knew he just had to dust himself off and get back in the game. However, this time it wasn't his tenacious attitude or blind determination to succeed that were mapping out his immediate future, it was simply luck. An extremely fortuitous encounter with a former singer-songwriter, who was now trying to make a living as an artist manager, would have a life-changing impact on Sam and their relationship would eventually shape the course of his career in ways he could never have imagined.

Sam had actually made contact with Elvin Smith a few years earlier, during the late spring of 2008, but their first encounter had been memorable for all the wrong reasons. At that time, Elvin was enjoying his first flush of success as a musician, touring and recording under the name Elviin. His big break had come when he was chosen as the opening act for Adele during her first high-profile gigs in the UK.

It's hard to imagine now, but at the end of 2007 Adele Adkins was still a relative unknown. Her debut single, 'Hometown Glory', had peaked at No.19 on the UK singles chart towards the end of that year and it was only following her second release, 'Chasing Pavements', when things really started to take off. That song climbed all the way to No.2 on the Official UK Singles Chart in January 2008 and signalled the start of her rise from obscurity to becoming a household name over the next few years. Adele's first string of tour dates took her from singing at small showcase gigs in venues like the Bloomsbury Theatre in London, with a capacity of less than 600, to playing in front of 2,000 fans at the Shepherd's Bush Empire in less than six months. Anyone lucky enough to be supporting her on the tour was enjoying a similar upturn in exposure and picking up scores of new fans along the way.

While it's hard to tell if Sam could actually be considered a true fan of Elviin at the time, it was during his set at the Shepherd's Bush Empire where the pair made initial contact. He recalled their first meeting in an interview with the *Guardian*: 'I was at an Adele concert, front row, Elvin was supporting her and I heckled him.' When asked if he'd taunted Elvin because his performance was bad, Sam stated, 'No. He's got a gorgeous voice.' Sam went on: 'He said something like, "This song is for someone I love," and I said, "Ah, thanks!" It was a nice heckle. Not abuse.' Sam admitted he'd had a couple of drinks that night and probably wasn't on his best behaviour. He went on to explain once he'd sobered up a little, he regretted what he'd done and felt embarrassed about giving Elvin a hard time. As soon as he got home that night he searched for Elvin online, contacting him via his Myspace page, and apologised. Elvin messaged back, but that was pretty much the whole of the conversation and ended their initial encounter.

Jump forward three years and Sam picks up the story: 'I went to a gig in King's Cross and saw [Elvin] there. I walked up to him and said, "You're Elvin, I saw you support Adele, I heckled you." He was like, "You're Sam Smith, I remember speaking to you on Myspace." And he was like, "I'm a manager now." It was too much of a coincidence.' The pair struck up a conversation, but Sam insists he hesitated and didn't immediately try to make any kind of professional connection. Rather than ask Elvin to be his manager there and then, for some reason he held back.

After the show had finished, Sam was smoking outside the venue when Elvin walked past on his way home. 'Something in my head told me, you've got to go for this,' Sam said. 'I ran down the street and said, "What's your email? I want to send you a song."' The song was 'Little Sailor' and it's safe to say the effect it had on Elvin was instant and fairly profound. Something within the lyric – someone giving everything they have to make their music dream come true and ending up scared the whole industry was going to chew them up and spit them out – resonated strongly with Elvin and he instantly felt a deep connection with Sam and his current situation.

Back in 2008, when Sam and Elvin's paths had first crossed, Elvin was riding high. Sam wasn't the only one who'd found Elvin's music on Myspace and he'd managed to build up a healthy following across social media and as a credible live act before signing to Virgin Records at the tail end of 2007. The Adele tour seemed like the perfect next step and it had, in turn, led to another tour, this time supporting her XL label-mate (and coincidentally a childhood friend of Elvin's), Jack Peñate. Shortly afterwards, Virgin were intent on sending Elvin to LA to finish recording his album with esteemed producer, Tony Hoffer, and suddenly things were shaping up nicely for his debut. There's no denying the calibre and eclectic nature of Hoffer's production credits, having already enjoyed considerable success working alongside Beck, Air, The Kooks and Supergrass, ahead of future collaborations with Depeche Mode, Goldfrapp, Ladyhawke and M83.

Having just produced Peñate's own debut, Hoffer must have felt like a good fit for Elvin's. The recording process had gone well, resulting in the completion of what undoubtedly felt like a decent enough batch of songs and the finished album, entitled *Made Of*, seemed both credible and commercial. The first track to appear was 'In Colour', a bright and breezy, piano-driven, pop-soul track which found its way onto the soundtrack of E4's drama series, *Nearly Famous*, and was playlisted at BBC Radio 2. Later, a flurry of media attention coincided with a limited, 7" vinyl-only release of 'In Colour' in May 2009 and Elvin found himself picking up a great deal of positive press. *Female First* declared, 'All hail the leader of the sunshine soul revolution 2009,' while the singer was also praised in the *Guardian*'s 'Artist of the Day' column. Drawing comparisons with Stevie Wonder, D'Angelo and John Legend, they noted, 'There's a crack in the voice, a nervous tremor, a note of anxiety in his positivity,' before adding, '[It] comes through every so often and hints that he's more than just another bland smoothie for wine bars.' But as the *Guardian* piece prophetically noted, 'Your success is never assured if you're a Brit-soul artist.' Virgin eventually decided to pass on releasing Elvin's debut album and he was subsequently dropped from the label.

For Elvin it was an understandably tough blow. It had been almost two years between signing with Virgin and any of the music he'd recorded actually being released. Frustratingly, in the meantime, a lot of the early momentum he managed to create had all but evaporated. Elvin eventually released his album independently, but he was understandably jaded by everything that had happened. In the end, without the backing of a major label, *Made Of* more or less disappeared without trace. Inevitably, Elvin's relationship with the performance side of the music industry soured very quickly after that. Although he toured again (supporting Alesha Dixon in late 2009), he knew he was fighting a losing battle and decided to use his experience elsewhere.

While he'd initially studied at art school, Elvin had also taken a course in accountancy and, although he had never officially qualified, the thought of combining his experience as an artist with the more business-minded side of his personality eventually led him into artist management. It's easy to see how Elvin's troubled past brushes with the harsher realities of the music business and the disappointments associated with never quite reaching your goal would help him empathise with Sam and his own rollercoaster ride with managers and recording contracts. If nothing else, he was an understanding and well-qualified shoulder to cry on. But it was clear there was something more substantial to their relationship.

Elvin had embraced a professional musical career relatively late in comparison to Sam. He was twenty-nine years old when his debut album was eventually released and he had only learned to play an instrument a couple of years before that. On a whim, he'd walked into a store selling musical instruments and bought a piano without being able to play a single note. It's a story that neatly illustrates Elvin's own passion for music and wilful determination, something akin to the hunger that drove Sam in his early teens.

Born in 1981, Elvin was a mere ten years older than Sam. And while the age difference was enough to give him the air of confidence and authority necessary for someone in his line of work, it meant he wasn't too far removed from all the things Sam was passionate about. Whether it was pop culture and fashion or an understanding of who, or what, was breaking on the music scene, the pair seemed to be pretty much in sync. But most of all, Sam respected Elvin as a fellow musician. Elvin shared his passion for making music and understood his need for self-expression and creative control over his music. Elvin's own attempts to make it as a live performer and recording artist meant he had a deeper understanding of the issues faced by every artist, especially new artists, when dealing with the largely unfamiliar, and often challenging, aspects of the music business. With all the coincidences and parallels pulling them together, it was hardly surprising that before long the pair had decided Elvin would indeed become Sam's seventh manager. And for the first time in a long while, things seemed to be moving in the right direction.

Previous experiences with artist managers and promoters had left Sam slightly jaded and wary of blindly trusting anyone involved with the music industry. Sam recognised Elvin's own rough treatment at the hands of the music industry made him a valuable and trustworthy ally. Over the years he had rejected the idea of dealing with anyone who was not going to be anything other than brutally honest at every stage of the journey they were about to embark on. Elvin had more reasons than most to empathise with Sam's need for transparency and clarity in terms of shaping his own future and he had no interest in feeding him false promises or selling him a fantasy he didn't think he could actually achieve.

But what truly characterised Elvin was his desire to see

Sam realise his potential as a singer-songwriter and someone who could shape the course of his own career by becoming a steering creative force within his own music. Almost immediately he had recognised that Sam was capable of more than just singing other people's songs, or being shoehorned into someone else's production. Elvin had a genuine interest in finding out what type of artist Sam wanted to be, encouraging him to keep writing songs and express himself more fully through his own music.

With 'Little Sailor' as a jump-off point, Elvin could see the potential in Sam as a singer-songwriter who could really connect with people. He heard a vulnerability and emotional honesty in Sam's voice when he sang, something that made him seem open and extremely relatable. If he could somehow harness these qualities in Sam's music, the combination of his voice and the right type of song would prove irresistible. He imagined hearing those powerful and affecting vocals fused with a song Sam truly believed in, and he knew the result would be something truly magical.

There were obvious parallels to be drawn between the type of songs Sam could potentially find himself writing and recording and the songs that had turned Adele into a worldwide success story in 2011. Adele's brand of confessional, emotionally exposed lyrics had struck a nerve around the world, turning her sophomore album, *21*, into a global phenomenon. The record would eventually become the biggest-selling album in the US for two consecutive years and in the wake of such unprecedented success, every label had been frantically hoping to sign 'the next Adele'.

Potentially, it made Sam a very commercial proposition,

and while the same comparison would eventually resurface when he did eventually begin to break through, Elvin made it clear from the outset that he wasn't interested in trying to turn him into anyone else. But while Elvin clearly had faith in Sam's natural abilities, and his aim was to help him fully develop his own unique voice and become an original and truly legitimate artist in his own right, he knew he couldn't do it alone. Sam was still a relative novice when it came to songwriting. Evidently there was the seed of something there, but it needed to be refined and nurtured. Elvin's first job as Sam's new manager would be to find him the perfect songwriting partner. Thankfully, he already had someone in mind and Sam was soon introduced to songwriter/musician/producer Jimmy Napes.

Born James Napier and raised in an artistic household in Camden, north London, Napes had already decided music was going to dominate his life by the time he'd turned fourteen years old. In some respects he was merely following in the footsteps of his musically minded parents. Napes' father, an English theatre designer working in the US, met his American mother while she was singing in the original Broadway cast of Andrew Lloyd Webber's *Cats*. Both played instruments – his father drums, his mother piano – and they had encouraged their son to take music lessons from an early age. Napes exceeded all their expectations and classical training in piano soon led to him learning both drums and guitar. His parents were less thrilled when he announced his intention to pass up the opportunity to take a university place in favour of pursuing his musical ambitions full-time. But as Napes told the *London Evening*

Standard, 'My parents didn't go to university either, so they didn't have a leg to stand on.'

Instead, at eighteen, Napes took a job in Los Angeles, working for a friend-of-a-friend at a company producing original music for commercials. As well as keeping him financially afloat, the job provided Napes with invaluable experience in creating music 'to order': 'It paid really well and taught me how to do lots of different styles of music.' When he eventually returned from LA, he had enough money saved to build a recording studio in a basement in London's Old Street. Harbouring dreams of mirroring the careers of his songwriting heroes, Carole King and Burt Bacharach, Napes' dream was to oversee his very own Brill Building, creating a mini-industry, writing and producing hit songs for other artists.

But things didn't quite work out exactly as planned and he found himself working non-stop for little reward. 'I was DJing at the weekend, just for like a job, but I wasn't making any money. I'd make like 100 quid or whatever just to see me through, but then I would just write all week. I was writing all the time, but I wasn't having any success with it.' Successful or not, his fortunes were about to take a dramatic turn for the better after a call from Elvin Smith.

Elvin and Napes' paths had crossed some time earlier and over the years the pair had become fairly close friends. Previously Elvin had used Napes' studio set-up and they were obviously keen to help each other out with work whenever they could. It was clear Elvin had a lot of respect for Napes and the thought of hooking him up with Sam Smith must have immediately struck him as a good idea. But with

Sam's relative inexperience as a songwriter, any potential partnership would inevitably fall at the first hurdle if he felt intimidated or overwhelmed by an overly domineering co-writer. It was unquestionably a difficult balance to achieve, but Elvin was confident he had made a solid match. Napes' unassuming nature and borderline shy demeanour might be misleading, considering his previous experiences in the music industry and his reputation as an accomplished, all-round musician, but it made him the perfect collaborator for Sam. Here was someone who shared his passion for music and eagerness to experiment, but Napes' lack of ego meant he was unlikely to pressurise Sam with his own agenda.

Elvin sent over a selection of Sam's work, which included his recording of 'Little Sailor', to test the waters and find out if Napes had any interest in working with him. Instantly, Napes was hooked. 'I heard Sam's demo and thought it was the best voice I'd ever heard,' he told the *Evening Standard*. Not quite believing what he was listening to, Napes pushed Elvin to set up a meeting with Sam. 'When he came to my studio I asked him to sing live what he'd sung on the demo,' Napes recalled. 'He did it even better than the recording.' It was immediately obvious there was instant chemistry between the pair. Napes again: 'We wrote "Lay Me Down" that day.'

The process Napes employed to break the ice with co-writers was one he'd perfected over many years. 'It almost always starts off as therapy,' he confessed to the *Evening Standard*, before elaborating on the process he used to put collaborators at ease. 'You sit and you have tea and you talk about life. Eventually someone will say something and you catch it, "We could write about that".' For Sam, the concept of injecting his own thoughts and real-life experiences into his songs was hardly new – 'Little Sailor' was a fairly transparent account of his current situation – but putting the theory into practice in partnership with other writers would be a revelation. It seemed to ignite something in Sam and proved to be a turning point in his growth, not only as a writer but also as a performer. It was Napes' belief that involving the singer in the collaborative songwriting process was fundamental to the emotional weight contained in the final song. The singer-songwriter who was willing to expose more of their true self in their lyrics would benefit from that connection when the time came for the recording process or performing their song in front of an audience: 'If people are engaged in what we're doing, there's much more chance of them understanding what they're singing, and singing with feeling.'

In the case of 'Lay Me Down', their first collaborative effort, there's a sense of catharsis, of Sam pouring everything he has into the song. Over a barely audible piano track, the song begins with a soft, almost whispered, urgently pleading vocal from Sam. As the track builds, he unleashes every trick he has in his impressive vocal arsenal. From the soulful croon he uses throughout, to the falsetto he'd been perfecting since he was a young boy mimicking his idols, 'Lay Me Down' was Sam showing anyone who'd listen exactly what he was capable of.

On the album's eventual release, US music magazine *Billboard* would praise Sam's performance on the track, saying, 'Within a single song, Smith runs the gamut of emotions he's been exploring throughout *In the Lonely Hour*, and seems to undo all the emotional work he had been doing to get over his heartbreak.' Meanwhile, *The Upcoming* simply described it as 'arguably one of the most heartbreaking tracks' Sam had released.

Similarly, Napes' skills as a multi-talented writer, musician and arranger are very much to the fore. The track's lush string arrangement gives a referential nod to Napes' beloved Bacharach, bathing the whole production in a glow of nostalgia without ever slipping into parody. But ultimately Napes wasn't interested in merely delivering a throwback to one of his idols – the track's overall sound was wholly contemporary and considerably more complex. *Billboard* would later say, '"Lay Me Down" has more of a theatrical flair than other songs, segueing from a Broadway musical's storytelling speak-sing to Whitney Houston's vocal acrobatics, to classy Frank Sinatra strings, to a sudden militaristic drum beat.' There was nothing straightforward about the structure or production, and the raw emotion in Sam's vocals made hearing the track for the first time an arresting and memorable experience.

If Sam and Napes intended 'Lay Me Down' to be their calling card, it was quite a bold opening statement. In just one song, the pair had created something that set them on a path towards a considerably brighter future and cemented a long and fruitful working relationship. For Sam especially, 'Lay Me Down' was a clear indication of where he was heading musically and seemed to perfectly encapsulate the style of music and type of songs he wanted associated with his name.

Eventually, that one song would open countless doors for both Sam and Jimmy Napes, acting as their bridge from 'struggling obscurity' to 'successful songwriters'. It was an impressive and assured co-creation considering just how recently the pair had actually begun their collaboration. It neatly showcased the strength of their creative chemistry, which had quickly blossomed during the writing and recording process, clearly demonstrating they were most definitely on the same page when it came to their shared passion for elegant productions and timeless songs. As Napes would later tell the *Evening Standard*, 'I always remind myself that I've written 995 rubbish songs and five good ones.' 'Lay Me Down' was definitely one of the 'five good ones' and it played a significant role in what happened next for the pair.

All in all, the writing and recording of 'Lay Me Down' would prove to be something of a landmark moment for the newly introduced pair. Their partnership would continue to blossom over the next year or so, Napes becoming heavily involved in the writing and producing of the majority of Sam's debut album. That record's eventual success saw him join Sam onstage at the Grammys in February 2015, where they picked up four awards for their work on *In the Lonely Hour*.

But at the start of their working relationship it was hard to imagine exactly where it would lead. Both had been chipping away unsuccessfully for many years before fate, or rather Elvin Smith, had brought them together. Rather than waste too much time fantasising about future fame and fortune, at the time of their meeting, Sam and

Napes were predominately concerned with keeping their heads above water. While Sam had his bar job, Napes was working on several outside music projects and here, it would appear that yet again, luck was to play an important part in Sam's story. Napes maintains he was very much on the outskirts of the UK's songwriting inner circle when his association with Sam began, forced to spend most evenings and weekends DJing in order to make enough money just to live on and spending every other free minute writing a seemingly endless production line of unwanted, and therefore, unheard songs.

The truth was slightly less bleak. Napes had plenty of other irons in the fire and whether or not he could actually be considered successful at this stage, he was making enough of an impact to secure the services of his own management team, Sam Evitt and Jack Street, at Method Music Ltd. Evitt and Street had used the knowledge and experience acquired from their previous jobs, working in marketing and handling artists under the umbrella of some of the UK's more established major record labels, to set up Method Music in 2010. Method specialised in looking after a wide range of aspiring musicians and artists, and while they'd signed Napes primarily as a songwriter, they were equally keen to utilise his talents in conjunction with projects involving their other signings.

Coincidentally, also on Evitt and Street's books were a couple of brothers named Guy and Howard Lawrence, who, under the name Disclosure, produced predominately dance-based tracks. The Lawrences were ambitious and multi-talented musicians, who, like Sam and Jimmy Napes, were desperately looking for their big break. Teaming them with Napes was a no-brainer, but no one could have imagined what would happen when Sam was thrown into the mix. The unlikely alchemy of a former ad composer, a teenage, diva-obsessed soul singer and two dance music connoisseurs was completely unexpected, but it was about to collectively turn their lives upside down and deliver the breakthrough hit they'd all been searching for.

THE DOMINO EFFECT

'He was born a famous singer. His personality doesn't suit not being famous. His aim in life is to work with Beyoncé.'
Howard Lawrence (one half of Disclosure) on Sam's
undeniable star quality *-Guardian*

Guy Lawrence was born on 25 May 1991, with his younger brother, Howard, arriving almost exactly three years later, on 11 May 1994. While they grew up in a time when the musical landscape was dominated by Brit Pop and Girl Power, where the likes of Blur, Oasis and Suede stood shoulder-to-shoulder with The Spice Girls, Steps and Robbie Williams in the UK charts, the Lawrence brothers didn't seem particularly interested in listening to the music being played on the radio then.

As Howard would later tell *Pitchfork*, the boys were raised in a very musical household and the genres of music they were exposed to covered a much wider spectrum: 'Almost everyone in our family has done music professionally at some point in their lives. My mum used to do radio jingles, my dad was in a band, and both my grandparents were musicians in orchestras and things.' In fact, both parents managed to make a good living working in different areas of the entertainment industry. Their dad was actually a member of several bands (sample names – No Angry Man and Look Book), which Guy, talking to the *Guardian*, would describe as sounding like 'Hall and Oates meets Led Zeppelin and Go West,' before adding, 'He looked like all the members of Duran Duran combined into one.'

Aside from working as session singer for hire, their mum fronted several bands, which performed at weddings and big social functions up and down the country. This had led to spending long periods of time touring as a singer on cruise ships and she'd even had a brief spell entertaining the troops during the Falklands War in the early 1980s. Growing up in this kind of environment, with a house full of musical instruments, it's hardly surprising the Lawrence boys seemed less inclined to listen to other people's music, preferring instead to make their own. 'Our parents got us into playing music,' Guy told *Pigeons and Planes*. 'We started playing instruments when we were very young. I've played drums and guitar since I was three years old. Howard plays bass and piano.'

As time went on they began looking outwards, keen to listen to others for inspiration. 'To be honest, when I was young, I rarely listened to music for enjoyment,' Guy admitted. 'I listened just to learn how to play my instruments.' And rather than developing their own personal preferences, the brothers' music tastes seemed to be dictated by more practical concerns, such as an eagerness to perfect their chosen instruments. Howard recalls, 'Guy would listen to prog rock that had amazing drumming in it. I was listening to funk and jazz because that music has the best bass in it.'

But by 2005, as Howard and Guy were about to enter their teens, the musical landscape outside the Lawrence family home was being transformed and things were definitely changing for the better. Music genres were beginning to merge and cross-pollinate in new and interesting ways, while UK dance and 'urban' acts were breaking through and pushing themselves into the mainstream like never before. Thus in the last five years of the decade, the likes of The Chemical Brothers, Basement Jaxx, The Prodigy, The Streets, Faithless, Gorillaz and, of course, Amy Winehouse all scored No.1 albums in the Official UK Album Chart. The UK's underground dance scene was also thriving, with an even more experimental and diverse array of artists and producers pushing the genre in unexpected and fascinating directions. And while Howard and Guy (as Disclosure) would find their spiritual home as dance music producers, this was never their original intention and at this point they were very much individuals whose interests and influences were still fairly distinct.

Guy told *Pitchfork*, 'We've never hated each other, but we didn't hang out much when we were teenagers. We were three years apart, which makes a big difference when you're at school. We didn't have many similar interests.' Howard would later elaborate in an interview with *Beat* magazine, 'Growing up we listened to pretty different stuff. I listened to more singer-songwriters, whereas Guy listened to more bands and American Hip Hop.' It was Guy's early affinity with hip hop, in particular the sound and production techniques pioneered by Detroit rapper-turned-producer J

Dilla, which finally led him, and eventually his brother, to start listening to more dance- and club-orientated records.

J Dilla was a true music pioneer, whose unique approach to sampling and the creation of beats saw him significantly change how US hip hop and R&B music was made in the mid-1990s. Before his untimely death in 2006, at the age of just thirty-two years old, J Dilla had become a prominent figure within the rap and hip hop community and his influence, direct or otherwise, could be heard in the diverse musical output of countless influential artists, including De La Soul, Common, Erykah Badu, Busta Rhymes and A Tribe Called Quest.

Guy told *Pigeons and Planes*, 'It wasn't until I was fourteen or fifteen when I started listening to hip-hop that I started listening for pleasure and got into the way that those guys made beats,' before confessing to *Beat*, 'I got into electronic music through that.' Over the next couple of years, he started to fully appreciate this previously unexplored avenue, before eventually being seduced by some of the more experimental artists emerging from the UK's burgeoning underground dance scene. It was dubstep, a new genre that had started to dominate the UK club scene, which would prove to be the most intriguing for him. An evolution of the much more frenetic drum and bass sound which had reached its peak a year or so earlier, dubstep incorporated elements of UK garage, reggae and dub, making it considerably more diverse and complex.

As the dubstep sound began to cross over, a host of UK acts, including Skream, Benga and Burial, were beginning to break through into more mainstream clubs. This coincided with Guy starting college and socialising a little more than he had in the past. Dubstep was a big influence on him. 'When I turned eighteen, that's what I started hearing in clubs,' he told *Pigeons and Planes*. 'Later, I went out to a few house raves and realized that house music was much more the type of music I wanted to make. So I went home and showed Howard. At first, we started out copying the people who were around then.'

Although it seemed to take a while for their music tastes to converge, it was clear Guy and Howard's individual desire simply to make their own music was the shared passion from which Disclosure would emerge. Howard would later admit to *Student Pocket Guide*, 'I didn't really know anything about dance music,' adding, 'I never really wanted to go clubbing until we started with Disclosure.' But he quickly came around to his brother's way of thinking, telling *Pitchfork*, 'That was the first time we were into the same music at the same time, which is probably why we started making it together.'

When the time came for the boys to pick subjects for their A-levels, both chose music and music technology, and it became apparent they were becoming increasingly centred on what they wanted to do. Howard told *Student Pocket Guide*, 'The other subjects we studied didn't really matter to us! All of our attention was focused on music.'

All things considered, it seemed almost inevitable the Lawrence brothers would eventually start collaborating on their own music project and soon the boys had embarked on a synchronised voyage of discovery into the world of dance music. Guy told *Pigeons and Planes*, 'We wanted to know where those guys who were playing modern house music got their sound from and what their influences were, and now their influences have sort of become our influences.' He concluded: 'Old Detroit techno, old Detroit house, old Chicago house, that's what it all leads to. If you get into dance music, you always end up there – listening to old house music.'

While the boys had settled on a very distinctive sound and production style, one seen as being more or less synonymous with dance music, they had doubts about the genre's limitations. Guy explained, 'It made us want to make songs in that format but not necessarily that type of music.' As Disclosure, the pair were less interested in pandering to the DJs who only wanted mixable club tracks, with extended instrumental breaks and endless breakdowns and build-ups. As Guy told *Dummy* magazine, 'We just forgot about that part of [dance] music and focused more on the structure of the songs and how to write melodies and lyrics,' before adding, 'Because we grew up listening to songs it made our music quite accessible.'

Without doubt, the boys were considerably more interested in the idea of applying the fundamentals of dance music production to a more conventional and therefore more commercial format. In an interview with *Metropolis*, Guy elaborated: 'We grew up playing instruments and listening to bands and listening to songs. We didn't grow up listening to instrumental dubs.' Initially uploading what they thought were 'rough demos' to Myspace, things started to move quickly. 'We thought we'd get some notes from people and make proper stuff after,' Howard confessed to *Billboard*. 'We were learning to make music, but every single got written up by blogs and released by an indie label.'

Thus, in August 2010, when Guy and Howard had just turned nineteen and sixteen years old respectively, they would release their first single as Disclosure, 'Offline Dexterity'. Receiving instant acclaim for their earliest recordings, the brothers began fine-tuning their own writing, recording and production set-up and quickly developed a fairly flexible and intuitive working style. Guy told *Pigeons and Planes*, 'Howard will do a whole song and I will mix it for him. Other times, I will make a whole song, sampling and everything, and then give it to Howard to see what he thinks.'

Over the next couple of years the pair released a handful of critically acclaimed tracks and EPs before their double A-side release, 'Tenderly'/'Flow', started to pick up significant national airplay and moved them onto the next level. From this platform, the band acquired a considerably larger and more mainstream audience. Along the way they'd joined Sam Evitt and Jack Street's Method Management and eventually signed a record deal with one of the UK's most esteemed underground labels, PMR.

Launched in 2011 by brothers Ben and Daniel Parmar, PMR had set out with a fairly clear agenda to discover and promote artists from the UK's underground dance scene. Ben had spent a long time working in A&R (Artist and Repertoire), signing and developing acts for some of the UK's major record labels, but had become increasingly jaded by the industry as a whole. 'Things had become really stale,' he told the *Guardian*. 'Big labels had completely lost their identities and I wanted to start a music company that had a real culture.' With this in mind, the Parmar brothers began signing similarly forward-thinking acts and shared their vision of what a record label could be. From conventional singer-songwriters and creatively-minded DJs, to the bedroom producers making world-class dance tunes on a relatively basic home-computer system, PMR's aim was to turn their acts into successful mainstream artists without necessarily removing their rougher edges or undermining their creativity and individuality.

'I guess the fact that I work out of the front room of my house with my brother and that all the acts on our roster have respect for and awareness of one another has been really important in allowing artists to be themselves,' Ben stated. 'It's created a unique atmosphere where everyone supports each other and attends each other's shows. I've never really experienced that before. I think it's quite rare.' He concluded, 'What we've tried to create is a family atmosphere where artists feel comfortable to be themselves.'

As relatively young artists who had a long way to go before they fully formulated which direction they wanted to take their own music, Guy and Howard were a perfect fit for PMR's more nurturing approach to artist development and promotion. Growing up, the pair had never assumed they'd make a living from creating and performing their own music. Indeed, their parents' careers had shown them there were no guarantees in the music industry. Both had been talented in their own fields and, as Guy told *Pitchfork*, they had 'managed to make a career out of music for many years, and they had a great time,' but they had never fulfilled their dream of really making it. Howard confessed to *Billboard*: 'We figured,

"If our parents didn't make it, why would we?" We thought we'd wind up session musicians.' But with PMR's help, the boys were beginning to realise the music they were already making could easily be taken in a more commercial direction, pushing them firmly into the mainstream.

While the industry taste-makers and credible music press seemed to want to pigeon-hole Disclosure as an underground dance act, Guy and Howard had other ideas. For them, there was no distinction between the music they made at the very beginning of their career and the tracks they wanted to make now. They simply saw it as a natural evolution, something that took them closer to the more straightforward and commercial songs they had always wanted to make. 'We grew up listening to bands,' Guy insisted to *Metropolis*. 'A lot of people get into producing dance music through DJing. We didn't grow up DJing or anything like that. We had a really clear idea together that we wanted to do something more than be DJs.' So, with Guy barely out of his teens and Howard having just left sixth form college, they were beginning to formulate a plan for Disclosure's immediate future and before long, with additional guidance from the teams at Method Management and the PMR label, they started creating a strategy for their debut album.

Ahead of Disclosure's signing and eventual breakthrough, PMR's biggest success to date had been with Jessie Ware, the south London born singer-songwriter who was nominated for the Mercury Prize with her 2012 debut, *Devotion*. Over the course of a few years, Ware's music had evolved from its underground roots to become an unusual, and considerably more commercial, hybrid of established soul and dance styles. With its distinctly contemporary and pop-orientated sheen, it was a clear indication to Guy and Howard that songs previously regarded as merely underground-friendly material could find a wider and more mainstream audience with limited compromise to their overall sound. That idea was neatly hammered home when they were asked to remix a track from Ware's debut album *Devotion*. The Disclosure remix of 'Running' was streamed over a million times across YouTube and SoundCloud, before becoming a crossover hit in several European countries during the late summer of 2012.

Like Ware, Disclosure's earliest material had found a receptive audience among some of the UK's most influential DJs and industry taste-makers. Subsequently, this saw the band mistakenly branded as simply being part of a wider underground dance scene, which included the likes of Four Tet and Burial. 'We love that stuff,' Howard stressed to *Dummy* magazine, 'but we were never part of that scene. They never embraced what we were doing, and I totally understand why, because we were making way poppier stuff than that. 'The misconception is that we were underground before. We weren't: we've always written pop songs.'

Guy and Howard's desire was to produce much more mainstream songs and after consultation with their newly appointed managers, the pair began to pull together the ingredients that would later form the overall sound of their debut album, *Settle*. Guy laid out their plans as follows, 'I would say that it's pop-structured songs, like a mix of verse-chorus kind of songs with vocals on them, and then instrumental club tracks, all written in the style of, and influenced by, house and garage from the 90s.' As a manifesto, it sounded fairly assured. And while their blueprint was something that would set them apart from most of their contemporaries, it would also eventually alienate them slightly from the underground scene that gave them their first break.

The pair were now fully committed to the concept of Disclosure being a predominately dance-orientated project, but with a pronounced pop sensibility. It would certainly be a difficult balancing act to achieve. If they wanted to produce a batch of songs which could gain mainstream acceptance through daytime radio play and still appeal to clubbers, those songs would need to cover a lot of bases, and their jump-off point would be finding a suitably eclectic bunch of interesting and creative collaborators. As well as pulling in some favours from songwriters and vocalists they already knew, Guy and Howard turned to their managers for help.

Pretty soon the team at Method were sending out requests for suitable collaborators and things started falling into place. The Lawrence brothers felt the artists they eventually worked with should be more than just talented vocalists, songwriters and musicians. They hoped there might be more of a connection in terms of meeting like-minded individuals who wanted to talk about their own passion and experiences with music and spark something more worthwhile. Howard told *Student Pocket Guide*, 'I wanted to find out what they were about just as much as I wanted to work with them.'

Coincidentally, at almost exactly the same time as Disclosure were starting to put their album together, Jimmy

Napes, who was also a Method Management signing, had just put the finishing touches to the demo mix of 'Lay Me Down', the song he and Sam had only recently finished writing and recording. Without warning, Napes sent the demo via e-mail directly to Evitt and Street at Method to see what they thought. Apparently keen to get their immediate and honest reaction, he didn't supply any extra details about Sam or where the song had come from. Later, when discussing Napes' mysterious correspondence with *Mediaor*, Street revealed, '[There was] no message, no subject, just the attachment.'

It would seem there was method in this apparent madness. As Napes himself would eventually tell the *London Evening Standard*: 'It was a game to see how long it would take before my phone rang. It rang in less time than the length of the song.' As soon as Street and Evitt heard Sam's voice, they were completely hooked. 'His voice, his writing,' Street told *Mediaor*. 'He's just incredible, there's no other way to say it.' Aside from instantly cementing Modest's interest in working with him, their first thought was to get Sam and Napes in a room together with Guy and Howard and see what happened. With future collaboration in mind, the Method team passed on some of Disclosure's early work to Napes. He was suitably impressed, stating, 'Their music caught my attention because it appealed to my love for house and garage while sounding completely refreshing and very much their own. I found myself digging out dusty vinyl of old-school garage records.'

While Napes realised Sam's taste was grounded in a completely different genre to the one where Guy and

Howard had initially made their mark, he was confident there was a direct, if fairly unconventional, connection to be made between their two worlds. The Disclosure boys' reverence towards the history of dance music, and an understanding of the roots of their preferred genre, made him think their hooking up with Sam – a similarly passionate enthusiast of old-school soul and jazz – might prove unexpectedly fruitful. Sam must have known writing and recording a track with such credible, up-and-coming new artists would be an excellent opportunity for someone with his relatively limited songwriting experience. Being a featured vocalist on Disclosure's debut album might just provide the break he needed, and could be a huge boost to his career. But at the back of his mind there was also a nagging doubt as he realised he was entering wholly unfamiliar musical territory. 'To be honest, I didn't know a thing about dance music until I met [Disclosure],' he confessed to *The Line of Best Fit*. 'I didn't understand and all I really know was pop and soul and jazz. I didn't understand when I was listening to club tunes with lyrics in it.'

Initially unsure whether his voice and songwriting style were ideally suited to a more club-orientated sound, Sam must have wondered where he fitted into this potential new partnership. But on hearing some of Guy and Howard's earlier work, he soon realised he had totally underestimated them and the music they were making. He couldn't deny there was a lot more to Disclosure than simply branding them 'just dance artists', and on finally meeting the two brothers, he realised they shared the same hunger to be heard which had been his driving force for many years. Sam told *Pigeons and Planes*, 'They are musicians, they're incredible. They are highly, highly talented at what they do. Obviously, they wanted their music to reach the masses instead of staying underground, I think.'

While Sam may have had every reason to be a little hesitant in the beginning, for Guy and Howard it was a lot more straightforward. When the Lawrence brothers heard his 'Lay Me Down' demo they were more than a little intrigued, as Guy confessed to *Billboard*: 'We were amazed he wasn't a girl.' Gender confusion aside, the brothers were blown away by Sam's voice and once they learned that he also had a hand in writing the song, they knew he was exactly the type of guest artist they were keen to work with. With so many connections linking Method, Disclosure, Jimmy Napes and Sam, it was merely a matter of making a couple of phone calls to bring everyone together.

With no time to think about what was happening, Sam was soon psyching himself up for his first meeting with the Lawrence brothers. To ease him into the process, Guy and Howard decided the best way to kick-start their new writing partnership was to use one of their previously recorded instrumentals as a starting point. After a brief search through their unreleased material, they selected a few suitable tracks to play during their first writing session. While it was a fairly novel approach to writing a song for Sam, he was instantly drawn to one particular track. 'They were playing this beat,' he continued, 'and I thought it was great. I thought it was wicked.' The track in question was something Guy and Howard had been working on for a while and had considered complete in its largely instrumental form. Guy told *Spin* magazine, 'We just wanted to make a song in 6/8, in that time signature. There's hardly any other timing in dance music than 4/4, and all we wanted to do is just make a track in 6/8. That's how it started.'

Howard went on to tell *Metropolis*, 'It was quite a long process in a way, because we wrote the instrumental over a year ago, and it originally had samples on it from an a cappella vocal that we just sampled.' With Sam gravitating towards the unusual qualities of this specific track, they decided to use it as the basic backbone of the new song they were going to create together. And, with Sam's help, Guy and Howard very quickly began knocking it into shape. Howard explained, '[Sam] was like, "All right, I need you to take the samples off of it." So we kind of just deleted the samples and we just wrote over the track. As soon as we took them off, we finished writing "Latch" in just a couple of days.' Guy told *Spin* just how impressed he was with Sam's input, and how quickly his contribution transformed their original track. 'He wrote all the vocals in a day. He killed it. It was amazing.'

While fine-tuning the track and completing the finished production took a little longer, for Sam it was a speedy and revealing process. Within hours of meeting Guy and Howard, he and Napes had taken a skeleton track and created something completely new and unexpected. Sam told *The Line of Best Fit*, 'We basically wrote a classic song on top of it that day, the first day I ever met [them]. It changed everything because it opened my eyes up to a whole new world of music.'

Things may have been finally coming together for Sam, but the reality of having enough money to merely survive in

London meant he was still working full-time and had to fit any music activities into an already busy timetable. Talking to *The New York Times*, he said his contribution to the recording of 'Latch' was no exception: 'I did that vocal on my lunch break from the bar.' While Guy and Lawrence were already lucky enough to be working full-time on their music, 'Latch' similarly felt like something of a game-changer.

While they were all in the room together they knew they'd created something special, but Howard and Guy were unsure what the public's reaction would be towards the song. Guy explained to *Billboard*, 'We thought "Latch" was too weird for the radio and not clubby enough for the clubs.' At first, they worried the combination of Sam's soulful, but unmistakably pop, vocal and more underground, electronic dance music might sound too unusual to a mainstream audience. 'There are club songs and then songs in the style of club songs, which is kind of what we make,' Guy explained to *Pigeons and Planes*. '"Latch" isn't really a house song, it's a song that's produced like a house song.'

Ultimately, if 'Latch' was deemed too subversive for daytime radio, it would not be widely play-listed and they might struggle to reach the broader audience they needed to turn it into a hit. Similarly, if the track was seen as too accessible and commercial, it might alienate Disclosure's existing fan base and fail to find any audience at all. In the end, their initial assumptions proved to be fairly wide of the mark and once the song's popularity rapidly began to outstrip everyone's early expectations, Guy changed his stance and rather humbly admitted, '"Latch" is just a strange song that people like.' In real terms, 'Latch' acted as the perfect blend of Sam's more traditional, soul-infused pop songs and Disclosure's earlier forays into the underground dance arena and as such became an extremely important opening chapter in their respective careers.

'Latch' is a groundbreaking and, in many respects, almost completely genre-defying song. While it obviously has one eye on the dance-floor, it is structurally and lyrically far more complex than the average four-to-the-floor club track. It neatly highlights an issue Guy and Howard had already recognised about modern dance music and hoped to resolve with Disclosure's future output. 'It's surprising how rare it is to find a dance act that can write a song,' Howard told *Dummy* magazine. 'They can write beats, and make an amazing club tune, but they have no idea how to write a song.' There was no denying Sam and Napes' contributions were crucial to the overall success of the track and the lyric (and Sam's vocal) were as much a part of what made 'Latch' special as the production or the beats.

Initial reaction to 'Latch' was almost entirely positive. After it received its first play on Annie Mac's BBC Radio 1 show, it was streamed more than 150,000 times in under a week on Disclosure's SoundCloud page. As everyone involved in the track's creation had hoped, 'Latch' seemed to connect with the mainstream pop audience as much as it did with the more serious-minded music critics and its universal appeal meant exposure for Disclosure (and Sam) was as likely in the broadsheets and credible music blogs as it was on entertainment gossip websites and the tabloids.

Michael Cragg at the *Guardian* said: 'A lot of songs are written about lust and the immediate rush of falling head over heels in love with someone, but few seem to sum up its deliriousness as brilliantly as "Latch". He added: 'It's a slowly unravelling ode to the thrill of wanting to figuratively (and possibly literally) latch on to someone else.' Describing Sam's vocals as 'full-bodied', he went on to praise the song's attempts at exploring a deeper and considerably more complex side of commercial dance music, while noting Guy and Howard's associations with their label mate, Jessie Ware, proved they knew 'a thing or two about songs that feel emotionally direct and intimate'. All in all, there was obviously something more interesting going on than the chorus refrains of 'Take me higher' or 'Tonight's gonna be a good, good night', which were typical of standard dance tracks.

Released in October 2012, 'Latch' was an instant hit across UK radio and entered the Official Charts inside the Top 30. Over the next few weeks it climbed steadily, before peaking at No.11 in its fourth week and eventually lingering inside the Top 40 for the next four months. In America, where 'Latch' was given a belated release almost 18 months after its UK debut, the song became a phenomenon. Unlike anything else on mainstream US radio at the time, it caused quite a stir. 'When we heard it, everyone here was slack-jawed,' admitted John Michael, a program director for LA-based radio station KAMP-FM. 'Listeners were immediately like, "What is that?!"' Speaking to *Billboard* in June 2014, he went on to say, 'Occasionally, a really special record cuts through the noise. "Latch" was that rare song that you didn't know you needed until you heard it.' He concluded, 'I don't even think it's reached its peak.' He was right. 'Latch' became a slow-burning, 'sleeper' hit in the US, eventually hitting No.7 at the beginning of August and spending almost a full year in the Billboard Hot 100 singles chart.

With the release of 'Latch' back in the UK towards the end of 2012, Disclosure's profile hit a new high. And with his vocal playing such an important part in the song's overall appeal and subsequent success, Sam obviously started to receive a great deal of extra attention too. Ironically, considering he had been fantasising about this moment since he was just eight years old, he felt slightly unprepared, confessing to BBC News, 'I had no idea "Latch" would turn into what it turned into.'

With Disclosure already a fairly established live act, even before 'Latch' had been released, Sam faced the daunting prospect of joining Guy and Howard on stage to perform the song for some considerably bigger crowds than he'd been used to. Around that time, he told *Interview*, 'A few years ago I had a weird relationship with performing live. I didn't enjoy it as much because the nerves took over.' It was something he was going to have to deal with fairly quickly because Disclosure had some high-profile festival gigs and a major UK tour scheduled to begin in early September.

Thus, only a matter of weeks after the recording of 'Latch' was completed, Sam experienced a real baptism of fire, singing the previously unheard song in front of over 50,000 people. He told BBC News, 'The first show was Bestival and I was a state,' and told *Interview*, 'There were so many people, thousands and thousands of people. It's been an amazing start to my live shows.' Then, within a couple of weeks of 'Latch' being posted on SoundCloud, he was joining Disclosure on stage to perform the song at London's Shepherd's Bush Empire in his most important live show to date. Considering how many times he had been forced to sit, in what he described to *GQ* as 'a shit seat', on the venue's top tier just to catch a glimpse of his own idols, it was quite an emotional and understandably nerve-racking experience but he felt he was slowly putting his residual performance demons to bed. 'I used to have a little whisky before I went on stage,' he quipped to *Interview*. 'I realised that could have slowly turned into something a bit more serious.' He acknowledged that the more gigs he did, the less stressed he felt. 'You get used to it,' he stated, 'you get more confident. It's confidence building, really.'

For everyone involved in making the song – Sam, Guy and Howard Lawrence and Jimmy Napes – it was a particularly sweet victory. Not only did the success of 'Latch' represent the end of their struggle to be heard, it stood as a clear reminder of everything they'd been through to get there. Jimmy Napes summed up their relief to *Fader* by saying, 'Sam was pulling pints, I was DJing at weddings, the Disclosure boys didn't have a pot to piss in. We had that fire in our belly to be like, "Let's make the best record we can make."'

'Latch' perfectly encapsulated one half of Disclosure's manifesto as represented by their upcoming debut album. Talking to *Dummy*, Howard Lawrence said, 'We wanted to get a balance between having fully vocal, more "pop" songs like "Latch" and [other songs] with a more clubby element. Because we do both of those things, and we wanted to make sure we got that across.' For Sam, it had been something of a whirlwind. 'It's been quick,' he told *Fader*. 'The first session with Disclosure I ever had we did "Latch". It was released a month or so after and then I was suddenly not in my bar job anymore, which was just crazy because I'd had two years of working full-time then suddenly went to doing what I had always wanted to do.'

He had found the collaboration process surprisingly easy and it had undoubtedly added an extra dimension to his songwriting. While there had always been an openness and vulnerability in Sam's songs, his growing confidence as a writer was helping him dig even deeper and fully express himself in his music. 'Things went so badly for so long,' he told the *Guardian*, 'and then suddenly it all just goes amazing. Honestly, I remember waking up one morning and it was all different.' The sessions with Napes and the Lawrence brothers had brought him so close to something he'd been working towards for so many years and he was convinced much of his ambitious streak had been captured in the recording. Listening back, he felt his drive and determination to succeed was almost palpable. 'I think you can hear it in my voice,' he told *The New York Times*. 'That song is one of my proudest moments.'

'Latch' would signal the end of a long period of insecurity and uncertainty, in terms of what Sam could realistically achieve as a singer-songwriter, and it gave him a clearer indication of where he might be headed as an artist in his own right. It was quite an extraordinary opening round for his move into the limelight. What he couldn't have imagined was another impending collaboration that would eventually give him a massive worldwide hit and resoundingly set his career onto the fast track.

CHAPTER SEVEN

WORLDS COLLIDE

'It's all well and good having success but I've got to be a real person...
That would be the best kind of success; if I can get through this and
still remain me and still have the same morals I've grown up with.'
Shahid Khan (aka Naughty Boy) on keeping his feet
on the ground – *Soul Culture*, September 2013

The release of 'Latch' effectively turned Sam's world upside down. Virtually everything about his day-to-day life changed in the immediate aftermath of the song's success and suddenly the pressure was on for him to make some very important choices about his future. By the end of December 2012, shortly after 'Latch' was certified Silver (indicating sales of over 200,000), Sam was no longer working at the bar; he'd played his first important showcase gig in London and was on the verge of signing a deal with a major record label.

Quitting his full-time job was a no-brainer. The momentum created by 'Latch' was enough to ensure that, for now at least, it made sense for him to concentrate fully on writing and recording some new songs. It was time to capitalise on the exposure he'd been given as part of the Disclosure record and by the end of November he had announced he'd be joining the line-up at the esteemed Blue Flowers Xmas Special at the George IV pub on Chiswick High Road in west London.

The Blue Flowers showcase gigs had become the stuff of legend. Since their inception in 2004, they'd offered music industry insiders, as well as a small paying audience, the chance to experience up-and-coming new artists in a fairly intimate space. The brainchild of former Universal Publishing A&R man, Chris Pearson, the event was viewed within the industry as a stepping-stone. Pearson's idea grew from his personal dissatisfaction with the type of places he was forced to visit if he wanted to see brand new artists perform live, and his general concerns about the limited number of appropriate venues able to cater for smaller gigs in London. He hoped his Blue Flowers showcase nights might be an alternative for artists already resigned to playing their first gigs in dingy basements and student bars, or if they were lucky, filling support slots in cavernous halls where the audience was more likely to be in the bar than near the stage during their set. Pearson wanted to give artists the chance to showcase their talent in the best forum possible and Chiswick's George IV seemed to fit the bill perfectly.

Possessing the vibe of a jazz club rather than that of a sticky-floored indie dive, the George's 200-capacity crowd were mostly seated at tables in the pub's main room, with room to stand at the back for latecomers and the inevitable overspill. Pearson told the *Independent*, 'It was more intimate, more personal. When someone came up and was good, it was really good – right up in your face and everyone around you experiencing the same thing. You can stand at the back of other venues and not get the same experience. Wherever you were in here, you felt it.' This was definitely the type of place Sam felt comfortable performing. It was an altogether more familiar environment than the huge, faceless festival crowds he'd experienced with Disclosure, no doubt taking him back to the times he'd spent performing alongside his old singing teacher, Joanna Eden.

The Blue Flowers gigs had a reputation for uncovering some of the UK's most talented young artists and had in the past given a helping hand to newly emerged acts as diverse and innovative as Jamie T, Laura Marling, Noah and the Whale and Jack Peñate. They had also given a select few the opportunity to see future mega-stars, such as Adele, Mumford & Sons and Florence + the Machine, in a smaller venue long before they were selling out stadiums around the world.

History would prove Sam's night in December 2012 was no exception, with everyone on the bill eventually being shortlisted for the Brits Critics' Choice Award or the BBC's 'Sound Of...' poll, two of the UK music industry's most respected and accurate indicators of promising new talent. Top of the bill was Laura Mvula, the female soul singer-songwriter who would be shortlisted for both in 2013. Joining her would be George Ezra, who would be placed No.5 on the BBC 'Sound Of...' list in 2014, and James Bay, the poll's runner-up in 2015 and also a Brit Award winner that same year. For Sam, the gig was an invaluable first step. Aside from giving him a chance to sing some of his own material in front of an audience for the first time, it was a vital step towards his own eventual breakthrough in 2014, when he too would win the Brit Award and top the BBC 'Sound of...' list.

This was an exciting time for Sam, but he would be the first to admit it wasn't all plain sailing. He was moving closer to an area of the music business that had been completely beyond his reach in the past. His recent success would soon open doors to meetings with important industry figures and he was on the verge of making the type of deals that would take him closer to the dream he'd been chasing since well before his teens.

For Sam, though, it was definitely a case of 'Be careful what you wish for'. He later admitted that he suffered bouts of anxiety during this period of enormous change and, for the first time in a long while, was worried and stressed about making the right decisions about his future. 'That was the only time when I was actually quite scared,' he admitted to *The Line of Best Fit*. 'We released "Latch", and the response to it, me and, of course, Disclosure, was so positive. People were talking about me after that song, which was great, and I kind of felt pressured a little bit.' Thankfully, even before things really started to take off, there was a solid support system in place around him and as things rapidly progressed, Sam started to build his dream team.

Aside from his close friends and family, he was getting much-needed guidance and support from inside the industry from the likes of Jimmy Napes, the Disclosure boys and the team at their label, PMR. Also, he still had Elvin Smith onboard as his manager. But almost inevitably, it soon became clear that he was going to need even more help if he wanted to build on the buzz 'Latch' had created, move his career onto the next level and successfully launch himself as a solo artist. Retaining Elvin as part of his core team, Sam decided to also sign with Method, which meant Sam Evitt and Jack Street now had the dubious honour of being his eighth and ninth managers, all before he'd even turned twenty-one years old.

The first thing they needed to do, to capitalise on the increased exposure Sam had received from the Disclosure record, was to make sure people realised he was an artist in his own right and to give them a taste of what to expect from him as a solo artist. Aside from his voice, Sam wasn't featured in 'Latch's accompanying promo video, and although it had provided a useful period of anonymity while he prepared for what was to come, he now knew it was time people got to see who he was and to hear him sing something more straightforward and typical of the music he might eventually release himself.

Sam told *Best Fit*, 'I knew that we had "Lay Me Down", and I knew that is where I wanted to be. Those are the songs I wanted to sing.' So, in order to give his curious new fans, who might be searching online for the name 'Sam Smith', something more than his association with Disclosure and 'Latch', Sam recorded a video of an acoustic performance of 'Lay Me Down' and, on eighteen January 2013, posted it online. At the time of writing, this version of the song has been viewed over eighteen million times on YouTube and it's safe to say, even the initial reaction was close to a phenomenon. 'The response to that song has completely blown my mind,' Sam admitted. '"Lay Me Down" is the reason I'm signed. That truly changed my life.' If nothing else, the simple piano and vocal delivery in the video proved he could definitely sing and the power and range he'd shown on the Disclosure record were real. Any suggestion he was a one-trick pony, or that the voice featured on 'Latch' had been manipulated or enhanced in the studio, was quickly dismissed.

But it wasn't only record company and label executives who were sitting up and taking notice. Sam (or more precisely his voice) had also captured the attention of another multi-instrumentalist songwriter and record producer who went by the name of 'Naughty Boy'. Born Shahid Khan and raised in Watford, on the outskirts of northwest London, Khan had adopted the name Naughty Boy and founded his own music production company, Naughty Boy Recordings, after a brief spell studying Business and Marketing at the London Metropolitan University. Initially working out of his parents' garden shed, Khan would eventually upgrade to a studio in Ealing, west London, but only after receiving a little help from two improbable sources – Prince Charles and the broadcaster and former DJ Noel Edmonds.

Immediately after dropping out of college Khan had applied for funding from The Prince's Trust, the charitable organisation set up by the Prince of Wales to specifically help young people get a better start in life. The Trust was impressed with his 'garden shed' set-up and keen to help him expand his business, awarded him a £5,000 grant. In the same year, he also appeared as a contestant on the Noel Edmonds'-hosted Channel 4 quiz show, *Deal or No Deal*. Despite admitting he'd never seen the show before he was on it, and having to film twenty-six shows before it was his turn to compete, he eventually won a jackpot of £44,000. 'Everyone was getting stressed about it,' he told the *Evening Standard*, 'but really you don't have to know a thing. It's just opening boxes.'

The money kept him in business for the next few years, allowing him to buy equipment for his studio and to start making his own recordings. Khan was a self-taught musician, learning to play piano by trial and error. He stated, 'I don't want to feel like I'm "trained" in anything... a piano isn't a machine,' before admitting, 'I never read the instructions.' Working with several (then) underground artists who have since gone on to much bigger things, Khan helped supply beats for early underground recordings by UK rappers such as Tinie Tempah, Wiley, Bashy and Devlin.

While living this carefree and somewhat maverick lifestyle Khan got to meet Emeli Sandé, a trainee doctor from Aberdeen in Scotland, who had travelled to London while trying to land a record deal. After hearing Sandé perform just one song, the self-penned 'Baby's Eyes', at I Love Life – a low-key music industry showcase for unsigned artists – Khan was convinced he'd witnessed the birth of a genuine superstar. He said: 'She captivated me. I felt like she was just singing to me.' Immediately he approached her and offered his services. Eventually he helped fund Sandé's many trips to London, picking up the bills for her B&B accommodation, and helping her as she wrote and recorded the majority of the songs which would secure her a record deal and form the bulk of her debut album, *Our Version of Events*. It was an unlikely, but mutually beneficial partnership.

Sandé told the *London Evening Standard* that meeting Khan was crucial to the success that followed. 'I was never cool,' she said. 'He definitely gave me a sound and musical identity.' Khan, meanwhile, said Sandé had had a sobering effect on him. He stated, 'She made me take myself a lot more seriously. The way I approached making music changed dramatically when I started working with her.'

The first fruits of their partnership saw Sandé provide featured vocals on a pair of Top 10 hits, with 'Diamond Rings' reaching No.6 and 'Never Be Your Woman' peaking at No.8, for UK rappers Chipmunk and Wiley respectively. The former led directly to both Sandé and Naughty Boy securing individual publishing deals as songwriters and encouraged them to continue their symbiotic working relationship. The result was Naughty Boy co-writing and producing the majority of Sandé's 2012 debut album, *Our Version of Events*. Powered by the tracks 'Heaven' and 'Next To Me', both of which reached No.2 in the UK singles chart, Sandé's debut went on to become the biggest-selling album of 2012 (and second biggest of 2013), eventually certified double platinum for sales exceeding two million copies in the UK alone.

After his songwriting and production work with Sandé, Khan secured his own deal with Virgin Records and by mid-2012 the recording of Naughty Boy's debut artist album, *Hotel Cabana*, was well underway. He stated after the success of *Our Version of Events* he'd received so many requests from artists eager to work with him that his studio began to feel like a hotel and from there the idea of a concept album, with all the featured musicians becoming guests at Naughty Boy's 'hotel', began to take shape.

While Khan is obviously a talented musician and producer, he doesn't sing or rap on any of his own songs and it was clear he needed to find an extensive list of guest vocalists to complete the album. He was especially keen to make a genuine connection with the artists he worked with. He wasn't particularly interested in recruiting artists who'd sing whatever he told them to, or recorded their vocals separately in a different studio without ever having met him. But most of all, he wanted to remove any pressure to work with big names just for the sake of having a superstar on his album. He told *Digital Spy*, 'I ensured that every collaboration I did (was) here in the studio with the artist. It wasn't that thing where the record label gets involved and organises it. It was very much the people I wanted to feature on the album.'

Naturally, first on his list was Emeli Sandé and their subsequent collaboration, 'Wonder', became the album's lead single, reaching No.10 on the UK singles chart in November 2012. As well as enlisting big names for his project, such as Ed Sheeran and Tinie Tempah, Khan insisted he wanted to find some emerging new artists and showcase some undiscovered UK talent. He told *Idolator*, 'That's important for me with this album, as well as writing with mainstream and known artists, is to present new artists. There's nothing wrong with giving Alicia Keys or Rihanna a big hit, but for the next Alicia Keys or Rihanna, giving them the big hit… it feels different.'

By the time 'Wonder' had peaked on the singles chart, 'Latch' was already a big hit and the idea of Sam joining Naughty Boy in the studio for a writing session must have made sense, especially as he seemed to fit the criteria for

Khan's preferred collaborators. But as always with Sam, there was an element of chance involved with his getting together with Naughty Boy.

As work continued on the album, Khan had already found the 'La La La' sample he wanted to build a song around. He imagined a situation where someone was being told their relationship was ending and rather than hear the bad news, like a child, they would stick their fingers in their ear and sing 'La La La'. He told *Radio.com*, 'You don't have to listen to everything you're told. Sometimes it's cool just to block it out and act like a kid.'

Khan had planned to develop the concept of the song further and take it into the studio during his next session with Emeli Sandé. But the huge success of Sandé's debut album across much of Europe meant she'd spend most of 2012 and 2013 on tour. With their schedules completely out of sync, he decided to sit on the idea for 'La La La' until Sandé was available. It was around this time that he first met Sam, telling *Idolator*, 'I bumped into him in the studio because he was working with someone upstairs. I just said, as I do with a lot of people, you just say, "Let's do something".' Sam would later admit to *Hunger TV* nothing about the session with Naughty Boy felt planned or forced: 'I went into the studio casually and did "La La La".' That 'casual' encounter would lead to the production of one of the biggest-selling records of the year and in May 2013, 'La La La' would give Sam his first No. 1 record.

For their writing session Sam and Naughty Boy were joined by Jimmy Napes and, as was now fairly typical, a discussion about the basic theme led to a fairly dark and considerably more complex structure than the song's title suggests. But, with a total of eight writers credited in its creation, 'La La La' was not going to be completed overnight. With so many people involved, the song was inevitably going to mutate and evolve into something else. So, it's easy to assume when Sam's contribution to the writing of 'La La La' was done and he'd finished recording all his vocal parts, no one really had a clue what the finished record would sound like. Between recording the song and its eventual release as a single, Sam was truly beginning to live the life he'd dreamed of since he was a small boy.

To fully capitalise on the success of 'Latch' at the end of 2012, Sam decided to officially release 'Lay Me Down' as a single in mid-February 2013. Released via Method and PMR through an independent distribution deal, on limited edition 7' vinyl and digital download, 'Lay Me Down' failed to make much of a splash commercially, reportedly only reaching No.128 on the UK chart, but with little or no promotion it wasn't expected to do any more than announce Sam's arrival as a solo artist and act as a stop-gap while he worked on new material.

In between writing and recording sessions, he announced he'd be playing his first solo gig – at London's St Pancras Old Church in April – as well as joining Emeli Sandé as the opening act on a handful of her UK tour dates. Also, during the early months of 2013, Sam took his first trip to Los Angeles, accompanying Disclosure and a host of PMR acts to the annual Coachella festival, where he performed in front of a large and enthusiastic crowd. The trip was a welcome break and in a video travelogue made by PMR, you can see he is enjoying the late-night revelry and the group's drunken exploits as much as his time on stage with Disclosure. This period saw Sam fully embrace the lifestyle of an up-and-coming pop star. He seemed determined to life to the full and to seize every opportunity that came his way.

'My concept,' Sam told the *Guardian*, 'is to live my life as hard as I can and then write songs about it. Suck every moment for what it's worth.' Part of this philosophy, though, saw him sometimes behaving rather recklessly, especially considering his status as a relative newcomer. He admits during some of his songwriting trips to LA, where the sole intention was to meet established co-writers and musicians, he would often stay out late the night before the session, get drunk and have a wild adventure, just to have something to write a song about. While this didn't always go to plan, it obviously seemed like a good idea at the time.

'La La La' was released on 19 May 2013 – Sam's twenty-first birthday. He celebrated by tweeting, 'LA LA LA IS OFFICIALLY AVAILABLE TO BUY & I am officially 21 and one year closer to dying haha.' Within hours of being made available to download, the song had already reached No.1 on iTunes own tracks chart. Sam's response was understandably ecstatic, as he took to Twitter to say, 'NUMBER 1!!!!!!!!!!! ON MY 21ST!!!!!!!! Thank you so much!!!!!!!!!!! I've never been this happy x'

Sam was further rewarded the following Sunday when 'La La La' was announced as the UK's No.1 single on the Official Charts Company rundown. The same day, he joined Disclosure on stage at Radio 1's Big Weekend in Derry, Northern Ireland, to perform 'Latch'. Sam found his

No.1 success somewhat unexpected, but obviously a very welcome turn of events. 'It's huge. Huge,' he told BBC News. 'That box has been ticked.' He went on to explain just how important it was for him to receive such validation early on in his career. 'It gives me the chance to settle down and concentrate on the substance of my music, already knowing what it feels like to be number one.' He added, presumably with a smile, 'I'd like it again, obviously.'

'La La La' went on to become the fifth best-selling single of the year, trailing behind huge international hits by the likes of Robin Thicke and Pharrell ('Blurred Lines') and Daft Punk ('Get Lucky'), but beating some very well-known global acts such as Katy Perry, Justin Timberlake and Pink. Internationally, 'La La La' was similarly successful, topping the charts in several European countries and hitting the Top 20 virtually everywhere, including peaking at No.19 on the US Billboard Hot 100 singles chart.

While their period in the studio was relatively brief, the promotion trail for 'La La La' was fairly extensive and it's easy to imagine that during the hours they spent travelling and working together, Sam and Shahid Khan must have had plenty to talk about. Without question, it was an exciting and enjoyable time for Sam, but there were challenges to overcome and important decisions to be made about his long-term plans for his career. Khan shared his concerns about new artists being swallowed up by the music industry and had so far managed to remain relatively anonymous and fiercely maintained his image as a more 'behind the scenes', svengali-type figure. As the two bonded during the writing and recording process, it seems likely his words of wisdom would strike a chord with Sam and echoed his own feelings about being seduced by the industry and the lifestyle it promoted.

'Coming into the music industry was scary for me!' Khan admitted to *Contact Music*. 'I view fame as a danger especially how much people want it yet not necessarily getting it, because it never lives up to the hype. Music doesn't have to go through the process of "I'm signed, I'm famous, I'm better than you, I'm special". Sometimes it can just be about art and the music and I wanted to be a part of bringing that back.' It would seem his thoughts were wholly mirrored in how Sam was dealing with his own escalating celebrity.

For Sam was part of a growing sub-culture in music. It was a movement which had begun decades earlier, predominately among US rap and hip-hop artists, but which was now so widespread that half of the biggest-selling tracks in the UK released during 2013 included a 'featured' guest vocalist. While some acts, such as Calvin Harris, David Guetta and will.i.am, used the process as a means to effectively 'brag' about the famous names stored in their iPhones, others, like Naughty Boy, Disclosure and the similarly dance-orientated Rudimental, were just as likely to use their status to nurture unknown singers and give emerging artists a platform from which to launch their own careers.

Thus, aside from Sam (and obviously Emeli Sandé), in recent years the likes of John Newman, Katy B, Jess Glynne and Foxes have all found success on their own after first breaking through as a featured artist on someone else's song. The practice proved to be extremely beneficial for everyone involved – from the specific artists and guest vocalist on the records in question, to the broader music industry in general. Artist manager James Merritt, who represents another such featured artist, Ella Eyre, told the *Guardian*, 'Record labels don't really want to take much of a risk these days. Twenty years ago they would have signed up loads of acts – it was like throwing shit against the wall and seeing what sticks. These days the budgets are much smaller,' before concluding, 'None of that happens now. People are scared of the first hurdle.'

It was a view shared by Amir Amor, a member of Rudimental, the act who would give Eyre her break with their No. 1 song, 'Waiting All Night', in April 2013. 'It's easier for labels to get someone out without spending as much cash – if it's a feature on someone else's record, then you're not really paying for it, you're getting the money from it. A&R can test it out and say to their bosses, "It's justified signing the artist."' There are also numerous benefits for the main artist. An act can gain a certain amount of prestige if big name acts are willing to work with them or, conversely, it could be used as a means of offering patronage and championing undiscovered talent.

But for those artists who, like Shahid Khan and the Lawrence brothers, were more interested in staying behind the scenes and concentrating on actually creating music rather than dealing with the fame and unwanted attention which so often accompanies success in the music business, it's a perfect solution. Khan, aka Naughty Boy, explained to the *Guardian*, 'You've got people like myself, Rudimental, Disclosure, and these are pretty much faceless artists, and it's a shift in the way the music business works.'

He went on to explain it reflected a change in audiences' expectations of what an artist should be and how they discovered new music. 'Music buyers don't necessarily need the face any more, but we need singers. I think it's a good thing for new artists.'

For the guest singers involved, it was usually a win/win situation. Sam told the *Guardian*, '[I] was able to perform and practise while not being the front man.' He elaborated on this in *Pigeons and Planes*: 'If you're a strong artist who knows what you want and is a strong songwriter/singer with a presence, oh my god it's amazing. It's literally just like practising before you do your own thing and the pressure's almost a little bit off. You're doing these incredible shows and practising your trade, it's a dream. He went on: 'Normally, you get signed and it's just go, go, go. You learn in front of everyone by yourself. But I've gotten to learn behind a screen.'

It was a sentiment echoed by the singer John Newman, who hit No.1 with his first solo single, 'Love Me Again', in July 2013, but who had earlier scored two Top 20 singles as a featured vocalist with Rudimental. He did no publicity for these earlier releases. 'I wasn't doing the interviews, I wasn't doing the press,' he explained to the *Guardian*. 'When I look back now, that's brilliant – because I learned from their mistakes and from what they did right. I had an insight into the music industry of how to handle it.'

The 'breathing space' delivered by the featured artist route was crucial for Sam. Not appearing in the videos for 'Latch' or 'La La La' had helped create an air of mystery around his voice and with it had come a degree of faceless anonymity. Indeed, he seemed incredibly grateful that, for the time being at least, he could sit on the Tube, unrecognised, next to someone listening to 'Latch' through their headphones, or walk unhindered through the crowd at a festival moments before he took to the stage with Naughty Boy to sing 'La La La'.

But similarly, he recognised there was inevitably a downside. With that unfamiliarity there was a danger people might assume Sam was just a session singer, drafted in to merely supply vocals and his actual contribution would be overlooked. Speaking to the *Guardian*, he was keen to stress he was grateful, but it was definitely a two-way street. 'These aren't other people's songs,' he stated. '"Latch" is as much my song as it is Disclosure's song and "La La La" is as much my song as it is Naughty Boy's. It may say "feature", but I wrote those songs with these people. It's a collaboration, but one person is showcasing the other because they're in the position to.'

Utilising everything he'd learnt from his experiences with Disclosure and Naughty Boy, Sam was feeling more comfortable dealing with some of the extraneous pressures that invariably went hand in hand with the more creative elements of his job. With some of that pressure easing, he was free to concentrate on fully developing his own songwriting skills and laying down broader strokes in terms of the overall sound of the music he was going to make in the near future. But he knew he wasn't quite there yet. He insisted working with other artists early on in his career gave him time to explore more diverse genres of music and helped him focus in on his own sound. He explained to the *Guardian*, 'I think being a feature is lovely because you get to practise your trade before you dive fully into something. It's also exposed me to loads of different types of music. I was going for an acoustic sound when I first started out, but having done "Latch" and "La La La", there's more of a reason to be limitless in the way I'm writing.'

If he had learned one important lesson from the past, it was not to rush into anything until he felt ready. Elvin and Method were giving him the type of good advice and guidance every new young artist needs. Furthermore, his association with artists such as Disclosure, Jessie Ware and Naughty Boy, all of whom had spent a number of years honing their craft, fine-tuning their sound and building a clear picture of the type of artist they wanted to be, helped him realise he shouldn't squander the talent he had or be in too much of a rush to sign the first record deal he was offered.

It's obvious the success of 'Latch' and 'La La La' hadn't gone unnoticed within the wider reaches of the music industry and Sam's name was undoubtedly at the top of several labels' 'most wanted' lists. As Rudimental's Amir Amor told the *Guardian*, 'Once you've had some success the label are going to want to run with it while it's hot, and that's a mistake. The artist had to be ready, otherwise they'll end up getting dropped and not getting the success they deserve.'

Seemingly, with these words ringing in his ears, Sam decided his priority was finding the right home for his music, rather than being swayed by false promises and accepting the biggest cheque. He realised there was a logic in trying to sign a major recording deal now, but he wanted to make sure it was with a label who shared his musical vision and career prospects. Rather than letting this early success go to his head, or make him think it was necessary to immediately launch his solo career, it would seem the opposite was true. Instead, the leverage he gained from his collaborations with Disclosure and Naughty Boy simply gave him the confidence to say, 'Not yet,' if the right deal wasn't on the table.

Thankfully, there was one label that seemed to understand exactly what type of artist Sam should be. Just as importantly, they were more than willing to wait, play the long game and make the best album possible with an artist they truly believed in. They would insist Sam should take all the time he needed to thoroughly explore and develop his skills as a writer and performer and fully deliver on the enormous potential they believed he had as a solo artist.

With no immediate pressure to sign a deal or release a solo record as soon as possible, Sam, and his management, decided to use the time to ensure the record they did eventually make was a true representation of him as an artist. If they got it right, the album should be a reflection of his life-long passion for singing and neatly pay tribute to the type of artists he'd grown up idolising. The overall production style needed to mirror the timeless quality of the artists he loved and the songs themselves had to express something of Sam's own thoughts and experiences. At this stage in the process, it seemed they had their work cut out for them, but in retrospect, it would seem Sam used this extra time wisely.

Over the next few months he would embark on a series

of writing and recording sessions that would help define him as an artist and ultimately shape the course of every song featured on his subsequent debut album. Perhaps more crucially, it allowed him time to relax, soak up every new experience and embrace what was happening to him. As he embarked on the next, hugely important stage of his career, there's no doubt he was fundamentally more prepared than ever to face his inevitable breakthrough.

bove left: Sam performs with Disclosure at the 2013 Coachella Valley Music and Arts
stival in California.

bove right: With singer Eliza Doolittle at *Esquire* magazine's summer party in May,
13 at Somerset House, London.

low left: The Disclosure boys Howard (left) and Guy Lawrence pose with Sam at the
pital Summertime Ball at Wembley Arena in June 2013. Sam provided vocals for the
o's single 'Latch', which was well received by critics and fans alike.

low right: Maverick Sabre, New Machine and Sam attend The Vinyl Collection
rated by Annie Mac and AMP 2013 in London's Leicester Square.

Above left: Sam Smith wins the Critics' Choice Award at the BRIT Awards 2014. Previous recipients include Adele, Jessie J and Ellie Goulding.

Above right: With pal Katy Perry at Soho Desert House with Bacardi in La Quinta, California in April 2014.

Below: A dream come true: performing with Mary J. Blige at the Apollo Theater in New York in June 2014.

Above left: Festival chic: Sam hits Glastonbury 2014 with singer Florence Welch.

Above right: Sam delivered a beautiful, stripped-down version of 'Stay with Me' at the MTV Video Music Awards in August 2014.

Below left: Backstage with Miley Cyrus at the 2014 MTV VMAs.

Below right: In October that year, Sam was presented with the Q Best New Act Award singer Foxes.

Above left: Sam Smith thanks fans at the MOBO Awards 2014 on an overwhelmingly successful evening that saw him pick up four gongs, including best male artist and best album.

Above right: Backstage at the 57th Annual GRAMMY Awards with good friend Taylor Swift. Sam picked up four awards – more than any other act that night.

Below left: Front row with the fash pack: Sam attends the Burberry Prorsum AW 2015 show in February 2015 and is pictured alongside model-turned-actress Cara Delevingne.

Below right: The gongs keep coming! Sam receives a BRIT Award for British Break-through Act at the O2 Arena in February 2015.

TAKE ME
TO NIRVANA

'I don't think about whether it's gonna be a dance record or a ballad or anything when I'm making music. I sit in the studio and I think, "How am I feeling today?" and I write how I feel. It's really, really simple.' Sam Smith on the 'simple' process of writing songs for his multi-million selling debut album – *Digital Spy*, May 2014

Nick Raphael and Jo Charrington know a thing or two about discovering talent. Raphael's career stretches back to the mid-1990s when he started as product manager, and then label manager, for London Records' dance-focused off-shoot, FFRR. Charrington has a similarly lengthy service record, having earned her break in the music industry working as a marketing assistant for Raphael at London. She had gone on to work as a PA within various other UK record labels and eventually moved into artist management, helping to put together and finally managing the boy band Another Level in the mid- to late-nineties. By 2001, Raphael had joined Sony Records, as managing director of its Epic label, and he needed a safe pair of hands to oversee that label's A&R department. Having briefly worked together previously, Raphael knew Charrington could handle the job and tempted her back into the fold.

Over the next ten years the pair signed and launched an eclectic roster of acts at Sony, including Lemar, Scouting for Girls, Paloma Faith, The Priests and Charlotte Church, as well as nurturing the early careers of several former *X Factor* contestants, including Olly Murs, JLS and G4. In July 2011, after Universal Music UK decided to re-launch the London Records imprint, Raphael left Sony to be appointed London's new label president, with Charrington joining him to serve as senior vice president of A&R.

Over the next year or so they started signing acts to the label, but had initially failed to find any artists with huge commercial potential. It was around then that Raphael heard Sam's voice for the first time. 'I remember hearing "Latch" and thinking, "No person can go through that many vocal ranges at one time without going through a computer",' he told *Billboard*. 'And then he played "Lay Me Down", and I remember getting in the car afterward, calling the business affairs guy and saying, "Whatever we do, we must close this deal".' It was a sentiment echoed by Charrington, who added, 'We've never heard a voice like that in our twenty years of working together.'

Within a couple of months, Sam signed a UK label deal with Raphael, under the London Records banner. While it's obvious Raphael and Charrington recognised something special in him, in real terms they didn't have much to go on. But despite the fact Sam's songbook was relatively light at that point, they felt he was an artist worth nurturing and were more than happy to take a back seat while he (and his team) managed the on-going evolution of Sam's sound and, eventually, his image. Yet again, it would seem luck was on

Sam's side as Raphael and Charrington soon had another major upheaval to focus on.

In late 2012, the music industry was experiencing a period of unprecedented change. EMI Records had effectively been dissolved, with various elements of the renowned company's labels and repertoire being bought and absorbed by the remaining major record companies. One of EMI's most prestigious assets, Capitol Records, was acquired by Universal Music and a decision was made to re-launch the label with a suitable fanfare in 2013. Capitol had become known as one of the most prestigious record labels of all time, the home of iconic artists such as Frank Sinatra and Nat King Cole in the 1950s, before eventually becoming synonymous in the 1960s with The Beach Boys and launching The Beatles in the US, before releasing records by world-famous acts as diverse as Diana Ross, David Bowie, Tina Turner, Crowded House and Iron Maiden over the next few decades. But the label had fallen on hard times in recent years after merging with another of EMI's labels, Virgin Records, and was a shadow of its former self at the time of the Universal acquisition. In the US, the label would be run by former Columbia Records chairman Steve Barnett and he and his team had a vision for the type of artist the label should be giving a home to.

Previously, Barnett had orchestrated the signing of Adele to Columbia in the US and helped steer One Direction on their road to global domination, and he had similarly high expectations for what he and his team could achieve at Capitol. Their roster soon reflected the label's ethos to sign artists who demanded creative freedom and self-expression through their work, boasting the likes of Katy Perry, Arcade

Fire and 5 Seconds of Summer among their earliest signings, as well as eventually becoming a safe haven for several more established, legacy acts, including Elton John and Neil Diamond. Lucian Grange, Universal Music Group's chairman told the *Hollywood Reporter*, 'When we acquired Capitol, we made a commitment – both to the artist community and to the industry – that we would revive this once-great label.' He concluded, 'I am enormously proud to see what Steve and his team are doing... The building is buzzing.'

What happened next had a direct impact on Sam's newly signed deal and contributed to the extended period of artistic 'soul searching' he enjoyed during much of 2013. As part of Capitol's broader plans for the international re-launch of the label, Nick Raphael had been earmarked as a suitable president for the UK division and a decision was made to move the UK-based London Records under the Capitol umbrella, where it would act as a subsidiary label. The ensuing period of internal manoeuvring and agenda setting seems to have resulted in a lighter release slate for Capitol during much of 2013 and the decision to delay the launch of the label's biggest new signings, Sam and 5 Seconds of Summer, until early 2014.

During that period of limbo, Capitol US's president, Steve Barnett, made time to fly to London and watched Sam perform at the Islington Assembly Hall. It would seem Barnett wanted to see for himself what all the fuss was about. He told *Billboard* he wasn't even halfway through the concert when he texted senior Capitol executives back in Los Angeles, saying, 'I'm watching someone who could change the future of this label.' Sam's position within the pecking order changed overnight and effectively his original contract, which covered the UK exclusively, was upgraded to a much more substantial global deal. In the process, the Capitol UK offices were jokingly re-christened 'the house that Sam built' by Raphael, and Sam's reputation as one of the label's main priorities for 2014 was sealed.

In real terms, the success Sam enjoyed at the end of 2012 and in the first half of 2013, ensured he landed exactly the type of record deal he'd wanted. It had brought Capitol to the table and they'd made it clear they were completely sympathetic towards his desire to try and make the best record he possibly could. More importantly, they were willing to wait for it. Capitol's supportive approach, allowing him to find exactly the right tone and material for his album, coincided with their own internal restructuring and rebirth. It gave Sam the opportunity to distil his own tastes into the songs he was writing and fully explore every musical avenue. Sam was determined to use the time he'd been gifted wisely and subsequently, with almost a whole year to fully develop his own writing style and musical direction, Capitol's understanding helped ensure he was 100 per cent committed to the songs he would record for his debut album.

Sam was scheduled to meet two of his favourite songwriters, Sia Furler and Linda Perry, in early May, with a view to collaborating on tracks for his album. Perry had become one of the most sought after writer-producers after a five-year stint as lead singer with the band 4 Non Blondes. Over the next couple of decades, she wrote with countless world-class artists and produced international hits for the likes of Pink, Christina Aguilera, Gwen Stefani and James Blunt.

Australian-born Furler had also started out primarily as a singer-songwriter (under the name Sia), enjoying a degree of success and building a loyal, but decidedly cultish fan base. But by 2010, following the release of her fifth album, *We Are Born*, she had announced her semi-retirement as a performer. Subsequently, she would become one of the world's most successful contemporary songwriters – supplying songs for albums by the likes of Rihanna, Beyoncé and former *Glee* star, Lea Michele – before making a triumphant return as a performer with her 2014 album, *1000 Forms of Fear*. That album won her three ARIA awards (Australian Recording Industry Association) and saw its lead single, 'Chandelier', nominated for four Grammys.

Sam was understandably excited about writing with both these artists, considering how many of his idols they had already worked with and the calibre of their output. But subsequent writing sessions in Los Angeles proved largely fruitless – none of the songs they wrote together appeared on Sam's album when it was released the following year. It's clear something wasn't quite going to plan. Sam was well aware he'd found his biggest audience within a specific genre of music. Despite the lyrical content of the songs, and the undeniable soulfulness of his vocals, both 'La La La' and 'Latch' were unmistakably dance records and they'd been widely embraced by club DJs and specialist dance radio stations before spreading to the mainstream.

Sam admitted he felt a degree of pressure to follow the dance-orientated route, as it was the genre that had given him his first taste of chart success. After all, it was hardly the first time an artist had opted for dance music to kick-start or revitalise their career. Back in 1995, no one had seriously questioned the logic or motives of Everything But The Girl's Tracey Thorn and Ben Watt when a Todd Terry club remix of their song, 'Missing', became the biggest hit of their careers and prompted a fairly radical change in musical direction. Almost completely abandoning the jazz-infused, acoustic pop which had dominated much of their musical output up to that point, the duo's next couple of albums fully embraced a more underground club sound. It notably paved the way for Watt's subsequent career as a DJ and producer, working almost exclusively in the dance music genre.

For Sam, it made sense to stick with something commercially proven and he told *The Line of Best Fit*, 'I've gotten into the music industry with this, but now do we stay safe and make an electronic record.' But at the same time, as he would later tell *Digital Spy*, he wasn't particularly interested in merely cashing in on his previous successes and he questioned the logic of making a certain type of record based purely on the idea that one genre of music might sell more copies than another. 'I did panic at first, but then I thought I'd rather bring out an album and five people like it than be making music that isn't me.' He began wrestling with the notion that his music should reflect more of his own tastes, which meant the album wouldn't necessarily fit into one specific genre.

If Sam was struggling to find the means to express himself through his music, and working with complete strangers – even if they were some of the most acclaimed songwriters on the planet – wasn't producing the expected results, the answer seemed remarkably simple and a lot closer to home.

He had little trouble opening up to Jimmy Napes at their very first writing session, during which they'd created 'Lay Me Down', and they'd pulled off the same trick working together with Disclosure and Naughty Boy in the sessions which created 'Latch' and 'La La La' respectively. Perhaps the answer was finding collaborators like Napes, who had more in common with Sam and could relate more readily to the things he was trying to say in his songs. The writing and recording sessions he was attending in the first few months of 2013 seemed to be pushing him a certain way, but he clearly hadn't really settled on what type of album he wanted to make. Things were further complicated by the fact Sam's personal life was increasingly affecting his general frame of mind and inevitably began to filter into his creative process. His emotional state was affecting the type of songs he wanted to write and, naturally, this had a knock-on effect in terms of the overall tone of the songs and even how he wanted to sing them.

During the first couple of years since leaving home, Sam had experienced some of the more ugly aspects of being a young, gay man in London. He'd witnessed the seedier side of the gay scene and the prevailing culture of casual sex and one-night stands was something he found largely unsatisfying and completely at odds with his more romantic nature. 'I'm a huge romantic,' he admitted to *Vibe*. 'I don't like putting everything on the plate immediately and I don't like when things are easy. I like being wooed and I like wooing people.' From the outside, it might have looked as if he was simply finding it hard to cope with being single and the ups and downs involved in finding the right person to start a relationship with. But in truth, he had a secret and the burden of keeping it was making him stressed and unhappy: Sam had already fallen in love.

In the wake of the enormous success of his debut, *In the Lonely Hour*, there was a great deal of speculation about the subject matter of most of the songs on the album. Its overriding theme of unrequited love and heartbreak seemed to be wholly grounded in reality, detailing Sam's own experiences and desires, and soon everyone wanted to know who the songs were about. At first, Sam was surprisingly open, acknowledging the majority of his songs were indeed largely based on things that had happened to him over the last few years and being refreshingly candid about his own sexuality and the fact that the person he'd fallen for was a straight man.

But Sam drew the line at revealing the true identity of the man involved. That may or may not have had something to do with the fact that at that time the man in question was in the dark about the part he'd played in the creation of Sam's music. It remained a well-kept secret. It was an extra pressure Sam clearly didn't need and it's obvious the weight of this burden was partly responsible for his lack of focus and indecisiveness in terms of the type of songs he wanted to write and record.

While there's no doubt he had a lot on his mind and wanted to express much of what he was feeling through his songs, there was a baffling contradiction between his intention to fully explore the complex emotions he was experiencing and the tone of the music he was actually making. Sam told *Billboard*, 'As "Latch" grew more and more, I was working with people who'd written Rihanna songs, and I'm going, "I want to make a Rihanna record." But then I'd go into the studio and just start pouring my heart out, because I was completely in love with someone, and they'd say, "Maybe you shouldn't give everything away."'

It appears that halfway through 2013, Sam had an epiphany. The two things which seemed to be causing some sort of creative block – his indecision about what genre his music should belong to and concerns about how personal and emotionally raw his songs were becoming – just seemed to melt away. 'Why should I have a sound?' he asked in an interview with *Hunger TV*. 'People ask me, "What's your sound?" but why should I have one? If I wake up one morning and I feel like I want to go out and dance, I'm going to write a dance song because that's how I feel. Whereas if I wake up and I feel completely sad and lonely, I'll write a slow acoustic song.' He concluded, 'I really want to be able to do that on my album.'

Raphael and Charrington, and the rest of the team at Capitol, had said they could hear the genuine soul in Sam's voice from the very first moment they heard him sing and remained confident their patience would be rewarded if they gave him time to find a home for that soul in his own songs. With his label 100 per cent behind him, it seems clear Sam was suddenly free from any pressure he might have previously felt about delivering a purely commercial record. He told *Hunger*, 'I made the decision and said, "Look, I actually don't care if this makes no sense to anybody and it all goes just shit, I just really want to put out an album that I would have listened to and that I will listen to and love as much as I loved all those female divas.'" Indeed, there was a breadth of musical and rhythmic styles in the records he'd loved growing up, and while he knew it didn't make sense to simply go into the studio and attempt to recreate an old-school Whitney Houston or Mariah Carey album, he also knew his record should show similar range. Considering his almost-phobic approach to male voices when he was learning to sing, it's perhaps surprising Sam admits to looking to the likes of George Michael, Elton John, Boy George and Michael Jackson for inspiration. 'These people didn't have a specific genre of music,' he explained. 'It was their vocals, their lyrics and their performance that strung everything together.' In conclusion, he said, 'I felt as a male singer it was time to hear someone that flits from genre to genre. I really wanted to take that risk with what I'm doing.'

In retrospect, it hardly seems risky at all, but Sam was demonstrating he understood the limitations of the market his record would eventually be released into and the more casual music consumer's often blinkered attitude towards what they listen to. 'We are in a world where people do like to put a title and a name on things, just to make it clearer to process in their minds what something is,' he continued. 'They have to be told it's this or it's that and I really want to destroy that. You don't need to call this pop, soul or punk, let's not put a label on it.' He concluded, 'Good music and good stories, that's what it's about.' It was hardly rocket science, but in terms of setting himself an agenda, he finally seemed to be making the right choices.

Sam admits his earliest attempts at songwriting were more emotionally guarded, telling *Interview*, 'As a youngster when

I started writing and stuff, I did actually write more from other people's perspectives.' But around the time he turned eighteen, he began to feel notably burdened by some of the things he was having to deal with – his parents splitting up, frustrations about his singing career and the more difficult aspects of his move to London – and he was finding it increasingly difficult to ease the extra pressure on his own. 'I discovered that writing the truth is really therapeutic and amazing,' he explained. '[Now] every single one of my songs is about something very personal to me and I could tell anyone what it's about, each song. Like a diary, basically.'

As Sam began to get more comfortable with the idea of using the songs he was writing as a means not only to express himself but also to ease some of the emotional strain, he started to fully embrace the concept. He would later tell *Vibe* magazine, 'It's me talking about my issues and getting them out in my music so I don't have to deal with them in real life. It's therapy.' For he knew just how important it was for people to feel an emotional bond with the music they loved. Since childhood, he had felt it himself, listening to the likes of Whitney Houston and Aretha Franklin. But now he was slowly beginning to understand that connection had as much to do with the singer as the song they were singing. Whether it was a euphoric vocal washing over you on the dance-floor of a busy club or the emotional punch delivered by a heart-rending ballad, the true impact of a song depended on the belief that there was a deeper connection between the singer and a song's lyric.

Sam was slowly coming around to the idea that the qualities he'd discovered in his voice at an early age, and fully developed over a decade or so, were perfectly suited to a more truthful and confessional type of song. Combined with an equally honest and raw vocal performance, he began to imagine exactly the type of artist he could become. He told *Hunger*, 'I want everyone to know that I'm not trying to create a character at all. I'm really careless and I don't think before I speak and I really just hope that people look at my music and look at me as someone who is just like them.' He wanted the people who heard his music to realise he was the same as them – he was a normal person, someone who shared their problems and experiences, someone who felt the same way as they did – and with a certain type of song, he knew the bond between him and the listener would be incredibly strong.

Sam explained in the *Guardian*, 'People like real life. Why do people like all this crap television out there? Because you're looking at what you can relate to. And music should be speaking about things you can relate to. That's the key.' It was with this attitude and a more focused agenda that he began to truly find his voice within the writing and recording process. He told *Pigeons and Planes*, 'I kind of feel like I've got this brand, this niche, this "Sam Smith" thing. And it's just picking things and people to write with in a certain way to make it beautiful,' before adding with a smile, 'I feel like I'm creating something specific now instead of just pissin' in the air.'

In an interview with *Hunger TV*, he explained how the process of creating 'The Sam Smith Thing' was often a case of trial and error, not unlike capturing lightning in a bottle. 'I've done so many sessions but there [have] only been a few that

I've really connected with, I tell them everything. I tell them more than I should be telling them probably, but we sit there and we talk about it and we write lyrics and melodies,' before confessing, 'Every single one of my songs is so personal; there are songs on the album that I can't be in the room with when people listen to it because it's so personal.'

As these early writing and recording sessions progressed he began to realise the importance of spontaneity, as well as the easy chemistry he was feeling with some of his collaborators and the effect a harmonious atmosphere in the studio could have on the songs they were creating. 'Every song I've used so far and will use are ones that come quick and naturally and I don't think about.' He went on: 'I tend to not even think about lyrics too much. I like my lyrics to be similar to the way I speak. I'm not well spoken and I haven't got a huge vocabulary of amazing poetic words but I like that, I like my lyrics to be honest and relatable, that's how I work. I just be myself and speak my mind and people help me to put that into musical form.' It was clear there was a lot of soul-searching involved in what he was attempting to create and he was genuinely trying to instil as much of his own character and emotions into everything he chose to sing.

Sam stresses at this point he'd never really been in a long-term relationship before and, in fact, had yet to be in the situation where someone loved him in the same way he loved them. But he was adamant that his lack of real experience was irrelevant and the type of romantic encounters he'd actually had were just as valid and meaningful. In an interview with *Pigeons and Planes*, he reasoned the only song he'd written at that point which overtly dealt with the subject of mutual love was 'Latch'. He said, 'All the boys that were in the room with me when we were writing had been in love, so I was really channelling something that will be.'

But going forward, he was determined some darker elements of being in love, and less-obvious relationship stories, would feature as prominently in his music. He said, 'All my other songs are about brief loves and one-night stands, which I try to find the beauty in.' During an interview with *V* magazine he would elaborate on the subject: 'The record is about the fact that I've never really been in a relationship before. It sounds sad, but I believe that the best songs are love songs, and I wanted to make it clear to everybody that unrequited love is a form of love. And even learning to love yourself. There are so many different forms of love. But we don't call it real love, do we? We say real love is when you're with someone.'

His mission was becoming clearer: he wanted to write about experiencing love in the broadest sense imaginable. By documenting rarely explored avenues of love and romance he hoped his songs might ring true with a wider audience – people who had been left heartbroken, but who may have been told what they were feeling wasn't valid, or those who had been unlucky in love and needed an understanding shoulder to cry on. Sam explained, 'My album is my statement. It's my message, saying, "I may never have been in a relationship, but I have felt love. I have felt pain and hurt".'

It would seem to be a classic case of 'write what you know' as Sam set about chronicling his own triumphs and misadventures in the lyrics of his songs. He would later tell the *Guardian*, 'I'm kind of sick of listening to albums about the turmoils of relationships, never having had one. So I wanted to write an album for people who have never been in love. I want to be a voice for lonely people.' In his current situation and state of mind, it's hardly surprising love, or more accurately unrequited love, was obviously going to become a recurring theme in the songs he was writing during this period. Ultimately, the idea of being in love with someone who doesn't, or can't, love you back began to dominate the majority of Sam's writing and recording sessions and the overall tone of the songs being created started to change. He explained to *Interview*, 'My album focuses on unrequited love quite a lot because I don't think it's spoken about enough in music. I've been through it myself and I found it hard to find songs that were about that, so I've definitely tried to make that a part of my album.' It would seem he had plenty to say about that particular subject and soon the lyrics of several of the songs that would later appear on his album began to show the depth of his feelings.

Never one to shy away from the more agonising aspects of his situation, Sam became increasingly determined to truthfully reflect everything he was dealing with. He told *Pigeons and Planes*, 'I personally feel that unrequited love is as strong if not stronger than real love because it hurts, and pain is what hurts the most. It's the hardest feeling you can get... this album is kind of proof.'

While the last thing he wanted to do was make an album of miserable songs, he was equally single-minded about the idea of conveying exactly how he felt through his music. 'I get really scared every day that I've written a really depressing album,' he confessed, 'but it's real. That's what's honest, and that's what's real… I document my life in my music. When I'm happy, I'll write happy music.'

'Happy', it seems, would have to wait for album No.2, as Sam began to build a stockpile of songs covering almost every possible angle on the subject of love, loneliness and heartbreak. Over the course of the next six months, he would meet some of the UK's finest songwriters and musicians and slowly his album would begin to take shape. The first fruits of what he, and his collaborators, had been working on for the first half of 2013 were eventually unveiled late that summer, and proved to be a tantalising glimpse of what was to come.

CHAPTER NINE

HAVE FAITH IN ME

'It's hard to explain. I just sing.'
Sam Smith on his process of 'just' singing –
Rolling Stone, February 2015

At the beginning of 2014, Sam told BBC News, 'My job is to live my life and to write about it.' If he was sticking with this mantra, the second half of 2013 must have supplied him with enough material to fill at least a dozen albums. Aside from fine-tuning the writing and recording process which would eventually provide him with the songs for *In the Lonely Hour*, he was being kept incredibly busy elsewhere. As the Disclosure boys prepared to release their own debut album, *Settle*, in May 2013, Sam's contribution to 'Latch' meant he'd become an essential element in the record's launch plans. Thus, he joined Howard and Guy Lawrence for much of their packed promotional schedule, which eventually led to the album hitting No.1 on the Official UK Album Chart in early June. As well as appearing with Disclosure at most of the summer's major UK festivals

– including the V Festival, Glastonbury and T in the Park – Sam joined the boys to sing 'Latch' on *Later... with Jools Holland*, accompanied them to the Mercury Prize Awards Show (where their album was nominated for 'Album of the Year') and sang at the band's landmark outdoor concert in New York's Central Park in August.

But it wasn't just his collaboration with Disclosure that continued to make extracurricular demands on Sam's time in the summer of 2013. The unprecedented (and largely unexpected) popularity of 'La La La', the song he'd recorded with Naughty Boy, was practically a phenomenon. The song's universal appeal saw it reaching the Top 10 virtually everywhere it was released around the world. As the 'La La La' video passed 100 million views on YouTube in early September, Sam realised the song's success had spiralled out of control and there was nothing he could do but hold on tight and enjoy the ride. He would take to the stage to perform his collaborations on numerous occasions throughout the rest of 2013, culminating in appearing on stage at separate Naughty Boy and Disclosure headline gigs at the O2 Brixton Academy during the same week in November.

In terms of his own career, Sam was hardly taking it easy. As well as the two shows at St Pancras Old Church in late April and his first solo show in New York at the legendary Mercury Lounge, he had announced his first headline tour. Scheduled for late September, he would play his biggest solo gigs so far, appearing at Glasgow's King Tuts, Gorilla in Manchester, Bristol's Thekla and London's Islington Assembly Hall. As mentioned earlier, it was at this London gig where Capitol's US president, Steve Barnett, would see Sam perform live for the first time and immediately start the process of signing him for a worldwide deal. But for Sam the real highpoint must have been the release of his first official EP.

The *Nirvana* EP was released in the UK on 4 October 2013. It consisted of four songs, two of which were recent compositions, a live recording from the St Pancras Old Church concert and a new, acoustic version of 'Latch'. Sam described the EP to *Pigeons and Planes* as 'an introduction to my world' before telling BBC Radio 1 the songs contained on the EP were more 'experimental' than anything which would later appear on his forthcoming debut album and showed different aspects of his range as a vocalist, his development as a songwriter and the broadening of his own tastes in music.

With Capitol in such a state of flux, and with big plans to launch Sam with a 'bang' the following year, it was decided the EP shouldn't be seen as his proper debut. It made sense, considering the exploratory nature of the material and, thus, the EP was not released through Capitol Records, appearing instead on PMR and promoted via an independent distributor. Sam was obviously keen to release something for his new fans and this set of songs seemed like the perfect introduction. Aside from his obvious excitement about the new songs he'd recorded, he was undoubtedly aware that, by the time the *Nirvana* EP did finally appear, a whole year had passed since the release of 'Latch' and for any new artist 12 months is a very long time in the world of pop music. Sam would later tell *Hunger TV*, 'I released (the EP) because I wanted people to see the growth of what I'm doing and my love for all types of music.' In real terms, songs such as 'Safe with Me' and the EP's title track show the earliest stages of his still-evolving songwriting technique and give a fairly clear indication of where his music was headed.

'Safe with Me', the first track on the EP, was definitely something of a departure. It would be the first song he'd released under his new set-up, which was not co-written with Jimmy Napes, and while lyrically it appeared to be in the same vein as 'Latch', it showcased a somewhat edgier production style than anything Sam had previously released. 'Safe with Me' was created during an early writing and recording session with songwriter-producer, Ben Ash. A former attendee of the BRIT Academy's Trinity College, dropping out after a brief internship at a record label inspired Ash to get into music production full-time. The release of a couple of acclaimed EPs secured a deal at PMR, where he helped supply beats and performed production duties for tracks on his label-mate Jessie Ware's debut album, *Devotion*. Working under the name 'Two Inch Punch', Ash quickly gained a solid reputation as an accomplished writer, musician, remixer and producer, which would later lead to collaborations with breaking artists such as Years & Years and Ella Eyre, as well as more established acts like Brian Eno and Blur's Damon Albarn. Like Sam, Ash had been raised in a household of classic soul lovers, but while Sam had become fixated on the big soulful vocals of female artists such as Whitney Houston and Chaka Khan, Ash was drawn to the likes of Stevie Wonder, Otis Redding and Donny Hathaway, before graduating to 1990s R&B-soul artists such as Keith Sweat and Tony! Toni! Toné!

The one thing the pair did seem to wholeheartedly agree

on was the quality of the voice and the songs themselves were paramount. Long before he'd even met Sam, Ash told *Fader*, 'The most important things for me are always the vocals and the songwriting. If someone has a really bad voice I tend not to listen to it. It can be a really great song, great production, but if the voice isn't great, it's lost me.'

While it would seem the combination of Sam Smith and Ben Ash was a match made in heaven, Ash had already made it clear he wasn't someone who was particularly interested in producing artists purely for financial gain. 'I don't want to work with pop artists,' he insisted. 'But if the right thing came about and I had an angle on it and I could make it something of mine then I'd go for it.' It seems Sam was 'the right thing' and it appears once Ash heard his voice on 'Lay Me Down' and 'Latch' he needed little persuasion to come on board. It was obvious there was an element of 'rising to the challenge' involved with this decision. As a leading proponent of the so-called 'lovestep' movement, Ash was definitely at the cool end of the spectrum, producing his own underground tracks and remixing some of the UK's most credible artists. Sam may have featured on a couple of hit tracks, but in real terms he was a relatively untested proposition.

In many respects the idea of a young, male vocalist whose passions were old-school soul and jazz, with a leaning towards timeless structures and classic love songs, was slightly out of step with everything else going on in the music industry. But Ash seemed to see this as something to get his teeth into. 'I think there's a lot to be said for a producer who can make something that's not seen as cool and make it actually good,' he declared. When Sam and Ash finally got together, the result was undeniably special. 'Safe with Me' is a near-perfect amalgam of the two distinctly different worlds – Ash's beats and sampled backing vocal arrangements are complex, almost surreal, and there is a dream-like, trip-hop quality to the overall production, but adding Sam's characteristically soaring soulful vocals and falsetto flourishes elevates the track and sets it apart from virtually everything else in his repertoire at that point. *So So Gay Magazine* noted, 'If you enjoy your pop laden with fast, itchy beats, reminiscent of the stuff Timbaland used to produce Aaliyah, then you will love this song. The song is a perfect balance between Sam's soulful, sometimes distorted voice and the beat which falls in and out of the song perfectly.'

The EP's title track was the second of Sam's recent compositions to see the light of day and yet again, it saw him working with new collaborators, this time in the shape of writing-production duo Harry Craze and Hugo Chegwin. Better known as 'Craze & Hoax', the pair had made an auspicious breakthrough co-writing Emeli Sandé's first solo hit, 'Heaven' and going on to write and produce her other No.2 hit, 'Next To Me', as well as performing the same duties on her collaboration with Naughty Boy, 'Wonder'. With Craze and Chegwin moving in similar circles to most of Sam's previous collaborators, it was perhaps hardly surprising the duo were pulled into his orbit during preparations for his own album.

The song 'Nirvana' is something of a revelation. Its backing track is surprisingly sombre and understated, with layers of synthesiser strings, effect-laden guitars and muted drums – bringing to mind the introduction of Maria McKee's 1990 chart topper, 'Show Me Heaven' – before Sam's vocals take the song in a considerably more soulful and contemporary direction. 'Nirvana' is reminiscent of recent R&B experimentalists, such as Frank Ocean and The Weeknd, building to an emotional and uplifting chorus, with Sam utilising the full power of his vocal range and capturing his most assured performance to date on record. Lyrically, 'Nirvana' covers familiar territory for him, describing an all-consuming, if fleeting, infatuation and surrender. Sam told *Interview*, 'There were four of us in the room and we all wrote it about things individually. It's about doing something at night-time, one night, and not worrying about commitment or worrying about anything else in life. It's about something – a person, a thing – taking over you and taking you to somewhere just for a little bit.'

Initial reaction to the song was overwhelmingly positive, with many reviewers stating the quality of the songwriting and production on show were seriously raising expectations for Sam's forthcoming debut album. *Fader* said, '"Nirvana" is all torch song, serious and deeply emotional,' before praising Sam's overall vocal delivery and stating he sang the song 'like he's overcoming adversity'. To top it all, Adele even tweeted a link to the song and gave it a resounding 'thumbs up', saying, 'This Sam Smith song is so, so good.'

Also included on the EP was a live version of another new song Sam had written with Eg White, 'I've Told You Now'. Francis White had been writing and recording his own music under the name Eg White for many years, first as part of a duo, Eg & Alice, and then latterly as a solo artist. But White had found fame predominately as a songwriter, having co-written and produced huge hits for several UK artists, including Will Young ('Leave Right Now'), James Morrison ('You Give Me Something') and Duffy ('Warwick Avenue') before becoming synonymous with the worldwide success of Adele's debut album, *19*, having written and produced three of its standout tracks, including the hit single, 'Chasing Pavements'.

If past collaborations were anything to go by, White was a perfect co-writing partner for Sam and 'I've Told You Now' would later prove to be a highlight of the *In the Lonely Hour* set. Recorded live at Sam's St Pancras Old Church gig in April 2013, the simple piano and acoustic guitar backing is eventually augmented by lush, sweeping strings, but it's Sam's voice that truly shines. Pure and unaltered, his voice takes top billing as he gives a mesmerising and emotional performance. Closing out the UK version of the EP was an acoustic recording of his Disclosure collaboration, 'Latch'. Stripped of its nervous, stuttering beats, with its electronic urgency replaced by a simple piano and string arrangement, the acoustic 'Latch' becomes far rawer, an almost painfully melancholy experience.

Sam explained his reasoning for re-recording Disclosure's track in this way, telling *Interview*, 'It shows the sentimental side, which sometimes doesn't cut through when there's a massive beat behind the track. The beat that Disclosure made is just unbelievable, and when you listen to that version it makes you want to dance; it makes you want to go crazy, and it's euphoric.' He added: 'Whereas I feel like the acoustic version tells the other story of the song, and that is a beautiful love song. I feel like it allows you to listen to the lyrics.'

Quite a transformation, it was testament to the skill Sam had developed in terms of not just singing, but interpreting songs and injecting an emotional intensity into virtually any lyric through his performance. It would be this quality which would filter through into almost everything he was about to record for his debut album and beyond.

The *Nirvana* EP stands as a fascinating glimpse into the on-going progress of Sam's songwriting style and his first tentative steps towards finding the tone and overall sound of his soon-to-be-released Capitol debut. As he came close to entering 'the lonely hour', the evolution from accomplished singer to confident songwriter and performer was almost complete. Over the next few months the songs that would turn his debut album into a worldwide phenomenon would be created and in the process a star would be born.

CHAPTER TEN

ONLY THE LONELY

'We all get a bit confused sometimes that you can only feel love with another person, but it's not true. You can learn to love you, and almost fall in love with your loneliness.'
Sam Smith on accepting the love which only exists 'in the lonely hour' –
Pigeons and Planes, January 2014

As 2013 ended and Sam began to think about the year ahead, he told *Pigeons and Planes*, 'It's overwhelming and it's a little bit scary in the sense of what's to come. The kind of work I'm going to have to put in this year, it's scary because it's a lot to do.' While the next twelve months were undoubtedly daunting, it was equally true he had been preparing for this moment for most of his life and an uncharacteristic calm seemed to descend on him as he prepared for the challenges he knew were just around the corner. Through countless hours of vocal training, and the sacrifices he and his family had made along the way, a determination to find his true voice had dominated most of his teenage years, and with it he'd developed an almost overwhelming desire to learn the means to fully express himself through his own music. Everything Sam was experiencing now, and was looking forward to in the near future, simply felt like the culmination of all the hard work he'd already put in. He said, 'I don't feel pressure because it's about the music. And I really just want the best platform for my music, my songs, and my record.'

Much of the previous year had been spent in building the team he believed could end years of false promises and disappointments, and finally crack the code which had kept him so frustratingly on the outskirts of the music industry and help take him to the next level. He told *Pigeons & Planes*, 'I found three unbelievable managers who've completely changed my life. And what they did is they made me kind of switch all my opinions in my head. I had thought that this industry was one way, but actually when you find the right people, it's a beautiful place.'

While his previous experiences had left him justifiably disappointed and frustrated, much of his long-held fear had subsided, to be replaced with an overriding sense of optimism, if tempered by a healthy grain of cynicism. Having reasoned he'd been afraid for too long, now it was time to take control. Sam said, 'I experienced a really horrible side to the industry of just a lot of rejection. I was very young and it upset me... for the whole of 2013 it was amazing and I was meeting so many nice people, having lots of luck, and it was great.'

With Elvin Smith, Method's Sam Evitt and Jack Street and his new team at Capitol around him, suddenly he felt ready to tackle the more intimidating aspects of the music industry and firmly put the past behind him. He told *Hunger TV*, 'Before I got involved properly in it I was scared of it.

But I think the best thing is absolutely everyone I work with is honest and lovely and I think that makes a difference.' He went on to say, 'There are lovely, honest people in the business but it is the luck of the draw. Once you've got the right team and the right family around you it's not as nasty as people make it out to be.'

It was in this frame of mind, buoyed by the confidence he had in his team and the sense of security they provided that he embarked on the real 'heavy lifting' needed to create an album's worth of material. He wanted the music he made to resonate with an audience, songs that might be thought of as timeless and classic and, more than anything, he was eager for every song on the album to be undeniably 'Sam Smith'. It had become very clear to everyone working behind the scenes, during the process of finding suitable co-writers and producers who would help him put his first record together, there had to be a spark of chemistry between Sam and his collaborators in the studio. Nothing worthwhile was ever going to come from him turning up to record someone else's song over an already created backing track. He needed to feel some sort of connection with the songs he was singing and that started from the moment he entered the studio with a prospective collaborator. Once the conversation started flowing he would know very quickly if it was going to work or not. If he was holding back or wasn't allowed the opportunity to open up and fully express himself, the songs would lack the necessary depth of feeling, he reasoned. Sam wanted the album to be intensely personal and confessional. He wanted every song to be brutally honest, not only about the things he'd actually experienced but also his frustrations and unfulfilled desires. Only then would the songs truly reflect his current, raw emotional state.

While his managers and the team at Capitol were keen for Sam to meet with as many writers and producers as possible, they realised the benefit of having a degree of consistency throughout the writing and recording process. The project's obvious cornerstone was Jimmy Napes. His bond with Sam, and the contribution he'd made thus far, had already been invaluable in the earliest stages of the *In the Lonely Hour* sessions. He'd helped guide Sam's developing skills as a writer, acted as the perfect sounding board for ideas and endlessly encouraged him when it came to experimentation in the studio.

Despite Sam working with several talented songwriters and producers during the long process of gathering material for his album, writing several exceptional songs and creating some very polished tracks, everyone involved with putting the final record together agreed the heart of the album lay in the songs co-created by Sam and Jimmy Napes. In an interview with *Sound on Sound*, Steve Fitzmaurice, the mix engineer and co-producer who would eventually play a large part in creating the overall sound of *In the Lonely Hour*, revealed, 'Jimmy and Sam had written four or five of the key tracks for the album, and everyone kept coming back to these songs and preferred their demos.'

It was clear these tracks would have an influence on the overarching theme of the record and set the tone for the songs chosen. Sam insisted it was these songs that were most evocative of the emotions he was feeling during much of the writing process, created from his brewing frustration and (sometimes self-inflicted) sense of loneliness and were utterly representative of the time and place they documented. As well as the unrequited love affair he was dealing with at the time, he wanted *In the Lonely Hour* to reflect his similarly troubled relationship with London – the city he'd called home for a number of years and which formed the backdrop for most of the experiences and emotions he wished to chronicle in his music. Sam told *Pigeons and Planes*, 'I think it's important to be inspired by different places when you write music. [*In the Lonely Hour* has] all been recorded and written in London.' He went on to say: 'There is a loneliness in London. I actually walk a lot around London. I used to do sessions, probably about a two-hour walk from my house, and then after the session I'd walk home. There's just a lot of space in London to kind of just be by yourself and take everything in, and I guess it helped in a way with the album.'

Now confident he had a good idea of what the general tone of the album should be, and with a fairly extensive list of songs to choose from, Sam and his team began the difficult process of deciding which ones would eventually make it onto his debut album. As with most artists recording their first full-length release, Sam had more songs than he needed and inevitably there would be a few of his personal favourites which wouldn't make it onto the finished album. While a few would become bonus tracks on special editions of *In the Lonely Hour* in different international territories, some would remain unrecorded and unreleased.

Among those that didn't make it onto the debut record

was the song 'Skies of Rain', which Sam sang as the opening number at his St Pancras Old Church gig and had performed live during several of his earliest concerts. He told *Press Party*, 'I love that song so, so much,' before speculating about a belated release. 'Who knows? Possibly one day on a "songs that didn't make it" album.' Also missing in action were Sam's co-writing collaborations with Sia Furler and Linda Perry. The Linda Perry song in particular was a favourite of Sam's, having been written after a particularly wild night in Los Angeles. He told *Digital Spy* it was the best song he'd written which wasn't on his record, adding, 'I love it so much… I'm actually going to use it at some point, and it's actually going to be in something.' In the process of deciding which songs would make it onto Sam's album, the long-list of songs he'd written was cut. In the end, it would only be the demos of the songs on this shortlist which would be turned into finished recordings and from these tracks the final album would emerge.

And as the recording process got underway in November 2013, Sam was confident they had the raw material to create something special but it was almost inevitable he would lose some favourites along the way. Songs that may have felt like a 'sure thing' at the start of the writing process could fall by the wayside if they didn't seem to fit with the rest of the songs on the album and, similarly, certain songs might come alive during the recording session and become unexpected favourites. The only thing Sam was 100 per cent sure about at this stage was every song he recorded with a view to forming part of *In the Lonely Hour* needed to feel like it was definitely a 'Sam Smith Song'. He told *V* magazine, 'I've written about

100 songs over the past year. You just know when you've written the right one, because it has that spirituality, it has that honesty and truth.' Explaining exactly what went into turning a song into a 'Sam Smith Song', he added, 'I'll write a song and think it's great because I'm concentrating on it so much, and then one day I'll write a song that just flows. It's those songs that always make the cut, because they have the spirituality in them. My music relies solely on the feeling. Just the feeling.'

In the end there would be no doubt about Sam stamping his personality on every piece of music he released under his name. Once the final selection of tracks had been made, he would share co-writing credits on every single track included on *In the Lonely Hour* and was heavily involved with every aspect of the writing, recording and production of the record, with Jimmy Napes making a similar contribution to all but four of the songs on the final track listing.

With Sam's Jimmy Napes' collaborations giving the album a distinctive, emotionally powerful central theme, the decision was made not to include songs just for the sake of using the material they'd recorded and risk diluting the effectiveness of those key tracks. Thus, the standard version of the album would have a playing time of less than thirty-three minutes. Undeniably, this is an unusually short length for an album released in the CD era, with most contemporary releases apparently keen to give the appearance of value for money and filling up the full eighty minutes' running time available on each disc. But Steve Fitzmaurice seemed to be speaking for everyone connected to the making of Sam's album when he told *Sound on Sound*, 'I like short albums.' Fitzmaurice went on to explain he thought credit was due to Sam (and his writing partners) for delivering short, concise songs and the general consensus was they were all the more direct and affecting because of it. He admitted, 'We tried doubling a chorus in one or two songs, and then it was like, "No, let's keep it short, so people will want to play it again".'

With only ten songs chosen for the final track listing, it was obvious there would be a few much-loved songs, which had been given finished productions but would not be included on the standard album. Among those were a few of Sam's personal favourites and it seems no one wanted them to go to waste. A few key markets would simultaneously release 'deluxe' editions of *In the Lonely Hour* alongside the standard 10-track version, while certain retailers (such as Google Play and Target in the US) were also given some of these bonus tracks to add to an exclusive format. In the UK, the special edition of the album included 'La La La' with Naughty Boy, the acoustic version of 'Latch' and two new, finished studio recordings.

The first new recording, 'Restart' was a fairly unexpected co-write between Sam and Zane Lowe. Although predominately known as a DJ, having presented several shows on BBC Radio 1 since 2002, Lowe was actually a musician first and foremost. Immersed in his native New Zealand's small, but fast emerging rap scene in the early 1990s, he had toured and made an album, only turning to DJing when he moved to London in 1997. He had been carving out a separate career as a writer, producer and remixer since the late 2000s. Already he had contributed, as a writer or producer, to several projects by the likes of Snow Patrol, Tinie Tempah, Example and Chase & Status, before hearing about Sam Smith and getting the chance to work with him.

Lowe told *Noisey Vice*, 'Everyone talks in music – about what they're working on, what they're hearing, who's hot.' He had heard who was contributing to Sam's album and how it was shaping up to be bigger than most people in the industry had initially expected. Lowe went on to explain, 'My manager said, "I'd really love to put you in the room with Sam." I said, "I'd love to. Good luck."'

When Sam first heard *the* Zane Lowe wanted to work with him, he was a little confused. He told *Digital Spy*, 'I was a bit sceptical when I first got the call, because I was like, "He's a radio presenter". But then when you get in the studio with him, I don't understand why he hasn't been making music in the pop scene for longer,' before concluding, 'You've just got to listen to him on the radio to hear how much he loves music. So why the f**k shouldn't he be in the studio, creating it?'

It wasn't long before the pair started co-writing and the first fruit of their time together was a song called 'The Lottery'. While that song failed to make it onto Sam's album, there was definitely enough chemistry between them in the studio to warrant another session. Lowe's invaluable experience, dealing with everyone from excitable pop acts to seasoned, serious musicians, meant he knew how to get the best out of everyone and those relaxed initial meetings created the perfect atmosphere for Sam's style of confessional songwriting. Discussing his experiences in the studio with Lowe, Sam joked, 'The funny thing is, when you're in the booth and he's speaking to you, it does feel like you're in a radio interview!'

Lowe expanded on the pair's working method with *Noisey Vice*: 'I presented him with the bones [of "Restart"] – the basic rhythm track, the chords. We sat down and after maybe half an hour we'd knocked that track up.' He added, 'Sam is the most open, amazing, honest, beautiful collaborator. He's an amazing writer… very gifted and instinctive with his writing… an amazing artist who loves the whole process.'

Once they'd played back their first attempt at recording 'Restart', Lowe revealed, 'He loved the track. I loved the track. Everyone was really happy.' Sam has stated he would jump at the chance to work with Lowe again, and listening to 'Restart' it's easy to understand why. By far the closest Sam has come to recording a straight-up, old-school soul song, 'Restart' is joyful and uplifting, overflowing with finger-snapping sass. With its stuttering percussion and layers of falsetto backing vocals, 'Restart' brings to mind a long-lost Luther Vandross track, uncovered from his career-defining 'Never Too Much' era.

The other new addition to most special editions of the album was another early composition, 'Make It to Me', a song Sam wrote with Jimmy Napes and Disclosure's Howard Lawrence. For Sam, 'Make It to Me' became the ultimate rallying cry, his declaration of intent and the perfect launching pad into the next phase of his career. Released briefly as a free download at the beginning of 2014, a few months before the release of his album, Sam described what the song meant to him to *Pigeons and Planes*: 'That is my link between this album and my future. I don't know what's gonna happen, but that song is basically my mating call.' He explained further: 'It's basically me saying, "I've been lonely, I've been hurt, and I've been in love with people who don't love me back. But now I'm saying, whoever you are out there to come and fall in love with me so I can write my second album".'

Although 'Make It to Me' doesn't feature on the standard version of the album, it acts as a fitting postscript, 'one last thought' to wash away the heartbreak and pain that's gone before. Its deceptive simplicity, beginning with Sam's vocals over a basic piano accompaniment, eventually explodes into a soaring gospel chorus, underscored by uplifting power chords, carrying a message of hope and longed-for redemption. The basic structure and sentiment is reminiscent of Brenda Russell's 'Get Here', mirroring the longing and hopeful optimism at the heart of that particular song. Famously covered by Oleta Adams on her 1990 album, *Circle Of One*, 'Get Here' had became a Top-5 hit on both sides of the Atlantic when it was adopted as an anthem for the families of soldiers serving in the Gulf War, which was taking place in Iraq and Kuwait between the summer of 1990 and early 1991. Sam's cry of 'You're the one designed for me/A distant stranger that I will complete/I know you're out there we're meant to be/So keep your head up and make it to me,' may only be to a phantom lover but the sincerity and anguish is as heartfelt as any prayer for the return of a distant loved one.

With the *In the Lonely Hour* track list sealed, recording complete and the marketing campaign ready to go, the only question now was, 'What should the first single be?' Steve

Fitzmaurice told *Sound on Sound* that, as far as Nick Raphael, Sam's record company chief, was concerned there was only one choice: 'The only exception to everyone preferring the songs Sam and Jimmy had written right at the beginning was the song "Money on My Mind". Nick decided that the latter song would be the first single, as it's more uptempo and could work as a kind of bridge between the "La La La" track and Sam's new material.'

Much of the public's first introduction to the solo Sam Smith would come via the first single from the album, and in that respect 'Money on My Mind' was a very important song for setting up Sam's future career. That particular song came together towards the close of 2013 and signalled the end of a particularly positive and creative period for Sam. Despite the uncertainty and frustration he was carrying as a result of his problematic romantic life, Sam was feeling fairly content during much of 2013. He has stated that with his management now augmented by the team at Method, finding the perfect record label in Capitol and the numerous like-minded collaborators who'd already helped him create some of his best songs to date, he was confident about his future and the prospects of really getting his singing career started with the album he was in the process of making. Any residual doubts he had about his place within the wider music industry were beginning to fade; he understood that the more ugly side of the industry could be neutralised if only you had the right support system in place.

Sam explained to *Digital Spy* how a prospective collaboration with an established writer almost managed to derail everything. 'I had two writing sessions booked in with someone in the music industry and on the first one we basically got into an argument and the person I was writing with was making music for the wrong reasons. I didn't get too angry, except he got quite malicious about the whole thing.' But Sam was more determined than ever to stay true to his original vision for his own music and the thought of compromising, especially on what would be his proper debut album, just wasn't acceptable. He continued: 'They hardly wrote anything and they were also about the material things. They were just looking for money. He was basically asking me to write a hit song, so I could buy him a new car.'

Sam had been very clear from the beginning, with both his management and his team at Capitol, that he didn't want commercial success to be the driving concern when it came to the making of his album. He told *Pigeons and Planes*, 'I just wanted to make it clear before I did this album that I write music to be honest and true and to document my life. I do not do it for money.' He told *Digital Spy* the decision to quit the session was easy and he had the full backing of his team: 'I remember just thinking in the moment, "I'm not going to do the writing session the next day with you, because this is just bullshit". So the next day I rang up Two Inch Punch and I actually went in with him and we wrote a song.' That song was 'Money on My Mind'.

While the song retains much of the brutal honesty indicative of Sam's lyrics, 'Money on My Mind' has a different type of fire in its belly. Although viciously condemning the materialism at the heart of the song's subject matter, it does so with Sam's typically unfiltered and no-nonsense attitude. Laying out his agenda within the first couple of lines, Sam sings, 'Don't wanna see the numbers/I want to see heaven,' before unleashing the killer chorus, 'No I have no money on my mind/Just love'. In its position as album opener, 'Money on My Mind' acts as the perfect link between Sam as featured artist and as a solo performer. Free of the more challenging romantic concerns of much of the rest of the album, 'Money on My Mind' feels like a far simpler, more straightforward and instantly accessible pop song and in that respect it acts as a perfect stepping-stone from Sam's previous big chart successes with 'Latch' and 'La La La'. Retaining the electronic pulse and stuttering beats of the former and the killer chorus of the later, 'Money on My Mind' has its sights firmly set on covering as many bases as possible, sounding equally at home on radio as it does on the dance-floor.

When released as a single in the UK, 'Money on My Mind' was an instant No.1, hitting the top spot during the first week of March 2014 and becoming a Top-40 fixture for the next four months. In the US, though, 'Money on My Mind' was not released as a single, instead forming part of the US version of the *Nirvana* EP when it was released there in late January 2014 as a stop-gap before the release of *In the Lonely Hour*.

Most critics who reviewed the album felt 'Money on My Mind' was a worthy first single, if a little uncharacteristic of what was to follow on the album, and accepted its function as a useful transitional song. *Consequence of Sound* praised Sam's vocals, saying, 'He's in solid control of his voice, utilizing his falsetto as punctuation,' while *A.V. Club* stated, 'Ripping synthesizers are laced with the best of both sides of Smith's vocal prowess, creating a searing party-rocking tune.' *Renowned in Sound* declared, 'This is a beautifully crafted song featuring a stellar vocal performance,' before adding, 'I guarantee that the chorus will be stuck in your head for days after a couple of listens.' In the *Observer* review, 'Money on My Mind' was highlighted as a perfect example of Sam's desire to chronicle his life and experience within his songs, calling it 'a compellingly meta song about being signed, about writing to order and pulling against the puppeteer's strings.'

While 'Money on My Mind' undoubtedly got Sam's solo career off to a blistering start, it was hardly typical of the rest of the album. It would be the handful of songs he had written with Jimmy Napes which would deliver the album's real emotional punch and hopefully draw the listener in and make them want to follow Sam on his musical journey. While the professional liaison between Sam and Jimmy Napes may have steered the course of the recording of *In the Lonely Hour*, it was an altogether more complicated relationship which cast a longer shadow over much of the writing and recording process, and eventually dominated the subject matter and overall tone of the majority of the album's songs. Sam's unrequited love affair became the overarching theme of the record and was particularly prominent in several of its key songs – 'Leave Your Lover', 'I've Told You Now', 'I'm Not the Only One', 'Like I Can', 'Life Support' and 'Not In That Way'. Among these, the first couple of songs undoubtedly pack the most devastating emotional blows and deliver their message via the simplest, most stripped-back arrangements.

'Leave Your Lover' was a song written by Sam and Simon

Aldred, and would eventually be recorded with the help of Jimmy Napes alongside his long-time production partner, Steve Fitzmaurice. Aldred, the lead singer and chief songwriter with British indie-rock band Cherry Ghost, was in the process of writing and recording a solo record when the idea of collaborating with Sam was first mooted. He was using his own solo record as a form of palate cleanser following the release of Cherry Ghost's second album, and was keen to experiment with more electronic instrumentation and move away from his band's predominately guitar-based sound. Aldred had also recently decided to publicly 'come out' as gay and wanted to explore the subject in several of the songs on his record. He told the *Guardian*, 'The album is mostly about embracing relationships and love, with a longing that's now tinged with reality, of being gay and singing from that perspective.'

With this in mind, it was clear he and Sam would have plenty of similar ground to cover and the resulting song is unapologetically candid and heartbreaking. Over a simple, muted acoustic guitar backing, Sam's vocals switch effortlessly from hushed whispers to soaring falsetto as he pleads with the object of his affections to 'Pack up and leave everything', before stating, 'You don't see what I can bring.' Recalling the session with Aldred, Sam told *Digital Spy*, 'I wrote this track in Manchester with Simon Aldred, who's actually a gay man himself and we got together and this song came so quickly. We were in his living room having a cup of tea and I was completely entranced by the chords. I immediately came up with that lyric, "Leave your lover, leave him for me". I remember feeling so proud that I got the word "him" in. We just put that down as a demo and it took about an hour to write.' Sam added with a smile, 'Then we went and got a bagel together!'

It set the tone for what would happen throughout much of the early writing process. Sam was increasingly in need of an outlet to ease the pressure of his current situation and he was finding a welcome catharsis in the form of this kind of collaborative songwriting. Talking about his need to get certain aspects of his relationship, or rather the lack of it, off his chest, he admitted to *Interview* he was using his own songs as therapy. 'When I was going through that, instead of searching for songs by other artists to relate to I could listen to my own music. I'd do a song in the studio and it would explain everything I'm going through so perfectly that when I went home and I felt down I could listen to that to make me feel better.' He concluded: 'It's a documentation of my life. I think it's just important to put it out there.'

'Leave Your Lover' shows Sam at his most powerless and vulnerable, perfectly summing up the overall theme of the album as a whole and setting the tone for most of his songwriting sessions. While still at the demo stage, Sam admits 'Leave Your Lover' was so delicate and simple it was almost overlooked as a potential cut for the album. He told *Digital Spy*, 'I played it to my label and managers the day after we wrote it… They heard it for the first time and they said, "Yeah, it's really nice," but never spoke about it again.' As the months passed, and it was nearly the time for the album's track listing to be finalised, Sam spoke up for the song. 'I just said to my managers, "I'm always going to root for this one song – it's my personal favourite." They were like, "Oh, I can't remember that one." Then they listened back to it and we all just became completely obsessed with it.'

It was another revelatory moment for Sam in his journey towards believing in his own skills as a commercial songwriter, admitting, 'That's a nice lesson to learn actually, because it means if I really like a song, I'm never going to let go of it.'

'I've Told You Now' had previously appeared as a live recording on the *Nirvana* EP and the album take retains its simple arrangement and much of its spontaneity. Sam told *Digital Spy*, 'This is the first ever song I wrote with Eg White. The version that is actually on the record is the first version – that's the demo we got mastered.'

The desire to capture the power and clarity of Sam's very first pass at the vocals for his songs would become a recurring issue in the recording process. While it often resulted in the scrapping of re-recorded sessions in favour of using first takes and initial demos, he was adamant it gave the recordings an authenticity and energy virtually impossible to recreate through multiple takes or studio trickery. Some vocalists might have been nervous about sharing these early takes, concerned about minor flaws in their delivery or cracks in the voice, but Sam insisted it added character and texture to the songs. In the case of 'I've Told You Now' he said, 'I actually had bad tonsillitis on the day I recorded it, so if you listen carefully you can hear my phlegmy tonsils, which is nice and pretty!' Another song touching on the album's main theme finds Sam finally boiling over in exasperation as he asks why the devotion he has shown hasn't been returned. As he sings, 'Why do you think I come round here on my free will?/ Wasting all my precious time/What the hell', you can hear the weariness, as well as the anger and disappointment in his voice. *Pop Matters* said, '"I've Told You Now" recalls the soulful acoustic songs of India Arie. Smith's voice perfectly mirrors the frustration of the lyrics, alternating between a floating falsetto and a raspy, empowered wail.'

While Jimmy Napes' influence can be felt in the production of this selection of songs, 'I'm Not the Only One' was the only other song from the 'Unrequited Love Song Cycle' which was actually co-written by Sam with Napes. The journey from original idea to finished song was not as straightforward as most of the tracks on the album, as Sam explained to *Digital Spy*: 'Jimmy Napes played the chords one day and I was obsessed with them. We wrote a completely different song on top of those chords and it wasn't very good, so we scrapped it. Then two weeks later, I just loved the chords so we returned to them, and then we wrote "I'm Not the Only One" in like an hour.'

Despite the protracted nature of its creation, Sam insisted 'I'm Not the Only One' was another example of something spontaneous and raw which just flowed out of him. 'In all my records on the album,' he said, 'this song came the quickest in terms of lyrics.' Within its lyrics we find him at his most gut wrenching and emotionally raw as he mirrors his own tale of longing and disappointment with a tale of infidelity and duplicity. Here, the protagonist is left helpless and heartbroken as he tries to make sense of his lover's betrayal: 'For months on end I've had my doubts/Denying every tear/I wish this would be over now/But I know that I still need you here.'

Most critics agreed 'I'm Not the Only One' was an instant

standout track on the album, struck by the maturity on display in Sam's songwriting, as well as by his vocal delivery. *Renowned in Sound* stated: 'For a twenty-two-year-old there is a lot of emotion flowing through his voice, he knows he has soul in his vocal and is switched on enough to use it,' before adding, 'It's hard to listen to Sam Smith and remember he's only on his debut, he sings like a seasoned vocalist.'

'I'm Not the Only One' had already entered the UK Singles Chart as an album track prior to its release as a single in August 2014, eventually climbing to a chart peak of No.3 and spending the next six months comfortably inside the Top 40. In the US the track was also a sizeable hit, reaching the Top 5 and being certified 3 x Platinum to signify sales and streams in excess of three million. Its commercial success was prolonged by the release of a single remix featuring a guest appearance from US rapper A$ap Rocky. It was quite a departure in terms of the original tone, and Sam's next foray into the 'Featuring' culture, which had given him his big break the year before.

Sam explained the thought process behind the new version of the song to *Digital Spy*. 'For me this sounded like a jazzy track, but Zane Lowe was actually the one who said, "Sam, this is a hip-hop track. You need a rapper on it." So he kind of inspired us to get a rapper on it and just show a different life to the music. He added: 'I've always said my music is genre-less, and I always want it to remain that way.'

The album moves on with 'Like I Can'. This was a song Sam wrote with Matt Prime, with the final album version produced by Jimmy Napes and Steve Fitzmaurice and additional production duties performed by some-time

Naughty Boy collaborator, Mojam. Prime was yet another new collaborator for Sam, bringing a wealth of experience writing for some of the UK's biggest pop acts to the table. He had cut his teeth penning hit songs for Blue's Simon Webbe, Liberty X, Natalie Imbruglia and Jamelia in the early 2000s and has remained at the forefront of his field, contributing to recent projects by the likes of Olly Murs, McBusted, The Vamps and Jake Bugg.

While much of the record dealt with a fairly intense and frustrating relationship, Sam felt the album needed to have a bit of light and shade and Prime seemed the perfect collaborator to bring more of a pop edge to some of the songs. Although 'Like I Can' is very much a part of the overall theme, it is slightly more upbeat and optimistic. Sam explained to *Digital Spy*, 'I needed a breath of fresh air on some of these records. Some of them are so intense that I had to put some songs in there throughout that would be a relaxing moment for the listener.' He went on to say: 'I do think about the album in terms of an experience – I want people to listen from start to finish. "Like I Can", for me, is just a little rest.'

As Sam sings, 'Why are you looking down all the wrong roads?/When mine is the heart and the salt of the soul,' in a surprisingly full-bodied vocal, before he unleashes the full force of his powerful falsetto, you are left in no doubt he is still feeling the pain of rejection. He told *Digital Spy*, 'It's still an intense lyric – the whole idea of it is jealousy – but it's fun to listen to and it was fun to write.'

On 5 December 2014, 'Like I Can' was released as a single from *In the Lonely Hour*, becoming his fourth Top-

10 single as a solo artist when it entered the Official UK Singles Chart at No.9. The song remained inside the Top 40 chart for the next twenty-two weeks and registered more than 400,000 sales and streams.

The second-to-last song that deals directly with the subject of Sam's non-love affair is 'Life Support'. It was written at a point when everyone at the label and within Sam's management team was more or less satisfied they had a very commercial record already in the bag. Sam recalled in an interview with *Digital Spy*, 'The album was pretty much done, so I had no pressure to write any more hits.' In the spirit of producing something which felt slightly more off-centre and experimental, he turned to his former 'Safe with Me' collaborator, Ben Ash, aka Two Inch Punch. By giving the track a little extra edge – what *Pop Matters* would later describe as 'modernistic ambience' – Ash creates a completely different soundscape in which Sam's vocals truly shine. Backed by a decidedly muted wash of electronic strings and an unusually nervous, jittery rhythm track, Sam's vocal on 'Life Support' feels positively woozy and dream-like in comparison to much of the rest of the album and signals the point of realisation for the rejected lover in the ongoing story. As he finally takes control of his own situation, he admits, 'This world is my world, this is my choice/and you're the drug that gets me through.' Next, he states, 'It's clear that you don't have a clue,' as he fully accepts the object of his affections may well be blissfully ignorant rather than merely withholding his feelings.

Sam told *Digital Spy*, 'This was the last thing I worked on with Two Inch Punch, actually. We came to the studio and he had the rough idea for the chords. I had complete freedom in terms of the melody and I think to this day it's one of the most interesting songs I've ever done.' Critical response to the song echoed Sam's idea that 'Life Support' was something a little out of the ordinary. *Billboard* stated, 'Smith's falsetto blurs words together until they eventually collapse against each other during the song's breakdown, which mirrors his own.' While *Source* were keen to point out the song's place within the overall concept of the album and how wholly representative it was of Sam's power as a singer-songwriter. They said, 'Sam's ability to be vulnerable and let fans into the depths of his yearning and desire is what makes the album work and is one of his greatest strengths.'

The story concludes with the song, 'Not In That Way'. This track, above all others, is probably the song which best encapsulates the entire *In the Lonely Hour* concept. Sam stated in an interview with *Digital Spy*, 'This could possibly be the most important song on my album. It IS "In the Lonely Hour". That is what it is. That moment, that whole realisation of loving someone and them not loving you back. Well actually, they do love you back, but not in that way.' 'Not In That Way' saw him working with another first-time collaborator. On this occasion it was Fraser T. Smith, one of the UK's most established and respected writer-producers, who co-wrote the song with Sam and produced the final version that appears on the album.

In his late teens Fraser T. Smith had won a scholarship to study music and dedicated much of the next decade to playing guitar in numerous bands and as a soloist. Eventually he became more involved with the writing, mixing and production side of making records during his long working relationship with Craig David. Smith had been introduced to an unknown David in 1999, joining his band predominately as a guitarist, before becoming a key collaborator during David's early 2000s breakthrough. By the mid-2000s, Smith had more or less given up touring and performing completely to concentrate on songwriting and production full-time. Initially working almost exclusively with UK urban and R&B acts, Smith served as a co-writer and producer for several emerging UK artists, guiding both Kano and Plan B through the process of creating their debut albums and eventually working with the likes of Tinchy Stryder, Jamelia and Taio Cruz.

Smith's big break came in late 2008 with the release of 'Broken Strings', the James Morrison/Nelly Furtado duet he had co-written with Morrison and songwriter Nina Woodford. The song would go on to be a worldwide hit and opened the floodgates for requests for Smith to work with several diverse and internationally successful artists such as Keane, Britney Spears, Kaiser Chiefs and Leona Lewis. His biggest success to date would come in 2011 when he co-wrote and produced 'Set Fire to the Rain' with Adele for her *21* album. That particular song was a huge hit around the world, eventually certified as 4 x Platinum in the US, and won a Grammy for the pair in 2013.

Working with Smith and creating 'Not In That Way' would prove to be a particularly rewarding experience for Sam, as he would later reveal in an interview with *Digital Spy*. 'I remember when I wrote this song I was nearly in tears, because it explained exactly what I can't explain to the person, but in song. I knew that person was going to be listening to that song, so in a way I was saying it to them. It was an amazing moment for me.'

It would appear the writing and recording of 'Not In That Way' was the moment Sam began to realise he needed to let his unrequited love go, and signalled the first steps towards finally telling the man involved that the songs were indeed about him.

While it sits somewhere outside the six tracks which illustrate the overarching theme of the record, the song 'Good Thing' is as much a part of the story as the rest. Another co-write with Eg White, 'Good Thing' was instantly one of Sam's favourites on the album. He would later describe it as simultaneously reflecting his lowest moment in the process of making the album and the turning point in accepting the reality of his situation. When he sings, 'I have made the decision, not to answer your calls/Cos I put everything out there and I got nothing at all,' it is as defiant as it is heart-wrenching.

Written at the point when Sam and his team had a fairly clear idea of which tracks would be released as singles, the highly personal nature of its lyric meant 'Good Thing' was clearly going to remain an album track. Sam confirmed in an interview with *The Line of Best Fit* that 'Good Thing' was the song that touched the rawest nerves during its creation. 'I was really sad when I wrote it,' he explained. 'I think that is the most personal song on the record just because I'm not even properly singing on it.'

Talking to *Digital Spy*, he elaborated further on the writing process with Eg White and how it would take his preferred method of working to extremes. 'With all the songs we did together, we wrote in a very odd way. We didn't actually start making music at the beginning of the session, we would sit and he would ask me about what I was going through.' He joked: 'Eg knows more about my private life than a lot of people do.' Keen to really make this particular lyric as painfully honest as possible, Sam admitted he virtually bared his soul to his co-writer. 'With this song, I showed him my text messages. I showed him some things I had been saying between me and another guy, and he was writing down everything I was saying. He started playing some music and the song was then basically already written.'

The actual recording of the song was similarly clouded by Sam's emotional state, as he told *The Line of Best Fit*: 'When we went into the studio, I was also numb when I was singing it. I wasn't trying to sing, and I think it's the most honest that I've been on the record.' For him it felt like the culmination of everything he'd been trying to achieve over the course of the whole record. Honest and raw, but without self-pity, there is strength in the singer's decision to let go of the 'good thing' that can never be, fight back and build themselves up again. Sam told *Digital Spy*, '"Good Thing", for me, is the darkest song on the record. If you actually listen to the vocal, I'm not even trying to sing or sound pretty because I'm so upset and sad. I kind of loved that and I feel like it really came across in the song.'

'Good Thing' also sees Eg White flexing his considerable muscle as a producer, keeping things downbeat and lilting for much of the track before the middle section's string arrangement, so romantic and lush it wouldn't sound out of place in a Rodgers & Hammerstein musical, explodes from nowhere as if to mock the Hollywood fantasy of the unrequited love story in the lyric. *Billboard* summed it up in their review by saying, 'Beginning with swelling strings that spill into a muted guitar line like a teardrop breaking (yes, it's that dramatic), ("Good Thing") is the real beginning of the end that *In the Lonely Hour* is all about. Here lie the first hints of trouble in Smith's relationship, from a dream that he was mugged outside his beloved's house to the worst realization that he dared think his love was reciprocated.' As with most of the songs on the album, it's pretty intense and undeniably more complex than the average pop song. But any doubts about the fact he may have made a 'depressing' album were overruled by the self-belief Sam had about the relatable qualities of the album's overall theme. Rounding out the album would be 'Lay Me Down'. As the first song he wrote with Jimmy Napes and considering its place as the launchpad for Sam's songwriting evolution, it offers a fitting end to the whole record.

But perhaps the album's real cornerstone, and the song which would send its sales into orbit around the world, was a simple ballad with a running time of less than three minutes. In real terms, it would be one song, 'Stay with Me', which would eventually turn *In the Lonely Hour* into the multi-platinum sales success and Grammy winner in the US. While its position as Sam's signature song was more or less instantly sealed on release, it didn't get there without stirring up a little controversy along the way.

CHAPTER ELEVEN

WILL YOU HOLD MY HAND?

'This is where my fire comes out.'
Sam Smith on songwriting as an emotional release –
The *London Evening Standard*, February 2015

Consisting of two verses and a chorus which is repeated four times over the course of its two minutes and fifty-two seconds running time, 'Stay with Me' is a deceptively simple song. Excluding repetition, 'Stay with Me' actually contains fewer than 100 words, yet somehow still manages to tell an emotionally complex and universally relatable story. The importance of what just one song did for Sam Smith's career should never be underestimated. 'Stay with Me' is more likely than any other to take on the mantle of Sam's signature song, in the same way Sting will be eternally haunted by (and presumably financially secure because of) 'Every Breath You Take' and Elton John by 'Candle in the Wind'.

'Stay with Me' was the second single to be released in the UK from *In the Lonely Hour*, yet seemed to prove that he was more than merely a singles act. Within the album's overall concept and the unrequited love story that sets the tone for the majority of its songs, 'Stay with Me' feels like the prologue. It bathes the whole album in the deepest blue and is the listener's introduction to Sam as the hopeless romantic, revealing his inability, or perhaps just his unwillingness, to deal with the realities of brief love affairs and casual encounters. Sam described 'Stay with Me' to *Pigeons and Planes* as 'the real heart and soul of the album'. While discussing the song's imminent UK single release with *Digital Spy*, Sam said, 'I don't want it to go to number one,' but then clarified: 'If it goes to number one that's great, obviously that's an amazing thing… I don't want to keep having to do that… it's just too much.' Instead, he saw 'Stay with Me' as something more crucial to the overall success of his album. He continued, 'My main aim for this single is I want it to sell albums, and I want people to listen to this single and think, "Wow, I wanna hear the rest of the record".'

Perhaps more significantly, 'Stay with Me' would also prove to be the song which most effectively sums up the less-is-more, economical recording process for the whole album and it was that simplicity which was, ultimately, responsible for it becoming a phenomenal commercial hit around the world. Producer Steve Fitzmaurice explained to *Sound on Sound*, 'The first time I recorded him, it was immediately obvious what an amazing talent he is. So when we made his album, the vocals were key. His vocals had to be at the centre, and we stripped away everything that got in the way.' Fitzmaurice went on to say, 'I've been lucky enough to work with some of the world's greatest singers, like Rod Stewart,

Tina Turner, Cher and Seal, and Sam is easily in the same league. 'He sings completely effortlessly and natural.'

Nowhere is Sam's instinctive interpretation and easy delivery more pronounced than on 'Stay with Me'. As the third track on the album, following 'Money on My Mind' and 'Good Thing', 'Stay With Me' acts as the bridge into the 'Unrequited Love Song Cycle' – the six songs at the heart of *In the Lonely Hour* which chart Sam's realisation that the straight man he has fallen in love with will never be able to love him in the same way – setting the scene and, perhaps, explaining much of his lovelorn behaviour.

The session that created 'Stay with Me' was almost exactly the same as countless others he had experienced over the course of writing the songs for *In the Lonely Hour*. Joining him at this particular session was, undoubtedly, his most comfortable writing partner, Jimmy Napes, and they were joined by William Phillips, an up-and-coming musician/producer and a long-time associate of Napes, who records under the name 'Tourist'. For Phillips, the 'Stay with Me' session would eventually lead to him signing with Disclosure's label and agreeing a management deal with the team at Method.

A self-taught musician, Phillips' earliest interest in making music came from a decidedly more analytical and somewhat 'boffin-ish' place. He spent hours soaking up other people's records in an attempt to learn more about the various types of electronic sounds and instruments they were using. He insists his method of making music is definitely more 'error and error' than 'trial and error', and he swears his songs are all the better for it. He told *Clash*, 'I never really wanted to have somebody teach me how to play. I love the fact that I taught myself, because I have made so many little mistakes along the way.'

His first couple of EPs, released in late 2012, caught the attention of the Method Music team, and subsequently they signed him, as Tourist, to Disclosure's own label imprint. As the pseudonym Tourist suggests, Phillips likes the feeling of unfamiliarity and exploring different genres in music and this has definitely been his driving passion ever since. His enthusiasm for experimentation and natural curiosity, about all types of music, makes him a perfect collaborator and it's hardly surprising he drifted into Sam's orbit. While he sums up his career as someone who's 'just lucky enough to write music that he loves and get paid for it', his skills are far rarer and therefore much more valuable. He admits, 'For some reason, my brain is wired in a way that I get immense pleasure from sitting in a room making sounds and listening to things,' before stating, rather more bluntly, 'Music is the only thing I am not shit at.'

The prospect of working with Sam and Napes came up when Phillips found out Sam's managers at Method, Jack Street and Sam Evitt, were also interested in signing him. Phillips told *Billboard*, 'They were like, "Before we manage you, why don't we do some sessions? We've got this guy Sam Smith and this guy Jimmy." So we sat in a session.' While Phillips must have felt a great deal of pressure for things to go well, he wasn't being completely thrown to the lions, having already collaborated with Napes on other projects. With the knowledge that they'd previously bonded while working on some of his earlier Tourist recordings, Phillips stated, 'We didn't have any expectations. We just wanted to meet each other.'

Thus, the trio were gathered at Timber Street Studios, a studio complex situated just off Old Street, a stone's throw from the world-famous Barbican Centre, right in the heart of London. It was a location Sam knew well, one he'd started to think of as a virtual home-from-home and somewhere he now felt extraordinarily relaxed. Over the previous twelve months, Timber Street had become an important base of operations for the writing and recording of his album. It was where he did the majority of his writing with Jimmy Napes, and a handful of the demo recordings for *In the Lonely Hour* originated there. Sam was comfortable in this particular studio set-up and had a fairly good idea of what the room's strengths and weaknesses were, and most of all, within this space, he felt safe, willing to let go and open up about his own experiences during the writing process. He told *NME*, 'It's an amazing studio. It's got, like, a massive control room… and we spent the day together.'

Phillips, in an interview with *Popsugar*, recalled the moment of inception for 'Stay with Me' – 'I went into the studio and there was a piano there. Now, I'm this really anti-social person and if there's a piano, I just go [and play]. I turn into this loser and it really annoys everyone except Sam.' He proceeded to put together a simple three-chord refrain, which immediately caught Sam's attention. Phillips continued, 'Sam was like, "Wow, what's that?" I played these chords and then Sam… I could see him writing melodies in his head with Jimmy, and Jimmy got on the drums.'

Sam confirmed to *NME* how the basic structure of the song

came together surprisingly quickly: 'I remember it all started when Tourist hit these three chords. It was unbelievable and Jimmy started playing the drum pattern. The song just flowed out of us, so naturally.'

For the song's subject matter, Sam was keen to explore some of his earliest experiences of moving to London and trying to find someone to form a connection with. He told *NPR*, '"Stay with Me", for me, is my own personal anthem to the "walk of shame" that we've all gone through. It's the feeling after a one-night stand of not wanting that person to leave, even if you don't love them and don't even like them. It's about having that body next to you.' It was a relatively familiar subject for a song, if seen from a slightly different viewpoint, but for Sam it was important to stress it wasn't something that should be thought of as an exclusively female concern. He stated, 'I wanted to say it from a guy's perspective, as well, because I think we forget sometimes that guys are emotional.'

The lyrics of 'Stay with Me', while deeply personal to Sam, express something universally relatable, mirroring the feelings and experiences of so many people who have since heard the song. A modern-day hymn for the forsaken and loveless, it perfectly encapsulates the loneliness and isolation that go hand-in-hand with contemporary city living and the overpowering need to share a moment with someone, anyone, who might just understand and want the same thing. With a basic idea for the lyric and overall message, Sam told the *NME* the song came together quickly: 'I think it took about thirty to forty minutes to fully write the entire song, with lyrics and everything.'

With the song almost complete in under an hour, Sam and his co-writers got straight down to the recording of the demo. He entered Timber Street's cavernous recording room and just started to sing. 'I remember being in the booth,' he told the *NME*, 'and I was singing the song, just singing it over and over again, and the whole song, the whole vocal, is just one take of my voice.' Later, explaining the uncluttered, exposed quality evident in his vocal delivery, Sam told Tanya Rad at *On Air with Ryan Seacrest*, 'I'm an emotional guy and I think, unlike a lot of men in the industry and in music, I'm willing to show that emotional side,' before adding, 'I don't have any bravado to put in front, and I'm just showing my raw self.'

While the writing and initial recording had felt instinctive, with everything coming together in a fairly effortless fashion, Sam couldn't help but think something wasn't quite right. He told the *NME*, 'I remember coming into the booth afterwards and just being like, "It's okay".' Listening back to the track, the three were in agreement: 'I think it's good... it's okay. It's not amazing.' Then Sam had a flash of inspiration: what about adding a gospel choir to the chorus? Obviously, there was no choir waiting patiently in the wings, so he decided to improvise. 'I decided to layer vocals on top of the song. So for the "Stay with me/All I need" part, I layered my voice, probably about twenty times.'

Suddenly realising what Sam was trying to do, Jimmy Napes joined in, directing Sam around the room to capture his voice in different corners of Timber Street's massive studio space. Sam continued, 'I stood in different parts, round the entire room and layered my voice more and more, harmonising, all that kind of stuff.' Once they'd completed recording the same section over and over, Sam stayed in the booth, admitting the first playback was extremely emotional. 'I remember asking Jimmy to play it back in my ears and he played it back and it sounded like a gospel choir and I remember nearly crying 'cos the whole song suddenly made sense. It was like that one touch just turned the song into... it sounded anthemic and so soulful and gospel-y. I just couldn't believe it.'

With the demo now recorded, and their day in the studio done and dusted, Sam remembers being desperate to let everyone hear what they'd created. 'I remember ringing up my management, the label, immediately saying, "This is the one".' He maintains 'Stay with Me' is a great example of how he approaches making music and clearly shows how his own songwriting style has evolved over time. Sam insists it is almost completely instinctive, a spontaneous feeling rather than something pre-planned or manufactured. He told the *NME*, 'I doubt myself every single day of my life, but when it comes to writing music the first idea that comes into my head, I run with because I feel it's right,' before adding, 'Some people take a while and analyse or doubt themselves and change things, but I feel if it's coming out of me, it's natural and that's how it should be.'

But the journey to turn the 'Stay with Me' demo into a finished recording wasn't over. In its most basic form, it was just a verse and a chorus, with a running time of under two minutes. In mid-June 2013, Nick Raphael, the president of Capitol UK, arranged for producer Steve Fitzmaurice to work with Sam and Jimmy Napes, initially to finalise the mixing of the 'I've Told You Now' demo Sam had recorded with Eg White. Shortly after work had been completed on that track, Raphael asked Fitzmaurice to join Sam, Napes and Phillips at a session with a view to enhancing the original 'Stay with Me' demo.

Fitzmaurice, an industry veteran who certainly knows a thing or two about making hit records, had served his apprenticeship at Trevor Horn's Sarm West studios in London, working closely beside mixer Julian Mendelsohn and Horn himself. Over the years Fitzmaurice produced and mixed countless successful albums and singles for major artists, including Sting, Tina Turner, Seal and Depeche Mode. More recently, he has had a hand in recordings by singers as diverse as Paloma Faith, Olly Murs and Wretch 32. Fitzmaurice told *Sound on Sound*, '[Raphael] asked me if I could go to [Napes'] studio as a more senior influence and encourage them to write another section. They tried a few ideas and came up with the organ riff in the middle eight, and Sam tracked some vocals over that as well. That became the new structure of the song.'

Afterwards, Fitzmaurice supplied a final mix of the demo and the song remained unchanged until the actual recording sessions for *In the Lonely Hour* commenced, later that year, with everyone now re-convened at RAK Studios, near Regent's Park in Central London.

But, if writing and recording the demo had been less than an afternoon's work, getting a finalised recording of the song proved somewhat more elusive. Fitzmaurice remembers the overall recording of the album was going well and Capitol were extremely happy with the songs they had heard so far, with the label particularly excited about the handful of demos Sam and Jimmy Napes had made of the songs they'd written together. 'Everyone also felt that "Stay with Me" was a key track, and many alternate versions were done of it,' he told SOS, 'But they kept coming back to that rough mix that I had done.'

Known as 'chasing the demo', it's a relatively common situation when the energy and spontaneity of the artist's first performance is captured during the demo process but is lost in the transfer to a finished recording. While modern studio recording is now so sophisticated, and every note played by the band or breath made by the singer can be moved, manipulated or erased at the click of a mouse, it's still impossible to recreate the special magic that is often unique to the very first recorded performance of a song.

By November 2013, Capitol felt they had about half the songs they needed to complete the album, although they were still unsure how to finish the demos Sam and Napes had made. Fitzmaurice recalled, 'The label had the idea of putting Sam and Jimmy in a room with a band and a producer. So I was asked to come in, once again as the senior party, and we went to RAK for a week.' While much of the demo recording had been completed using keyboards, electronic sounds, drum machines and sampled beats and loops, it was thought Sam's performance might be enhanced with the feel of real instruments and singing along with live musicians. Thus a couple of members of Sam's live band, Reuben James and Ben Thomas, were enlisted to play piano and guitar respectively, and Fitzmaurice supplied session players, Earl Harvin and Jodi Milliner, to supply drums and bass.

Fitzmaurice remembers how the band quickly slipped into an incredibly productive routine. 'We'd listen to the song in the morning with the band, we'd talk about how we'd approach the song. After this we would play it through a few times without Sam, making sure everyone was happy.' Then, Sam's arrival at the studio signalled lunchtime and afterwards the whole band would settle in for the afternoon's recording.

Fitzmaurice continued, 'We'd then play the song through three or four times with [Sam] singing in the same room as the piano player, in a booth behind screens. And that would be it. That would be the song.' He concluded, 'We recorded seven songs in five days at RAK, most of them more or less finished, including yet another stab at recording "Stay with Me".'

The version recorded here was basically a carbon copy of the original demo. 'We knew that everyone loved the other version,' recalled Fitzmaurice. 'So we recorded a new version at the same tempo, and added some strings to that. But everyone once again still preferred the demo version!' Fitzmaurice and Napes then decided to create what they called a 'hybrid' mix, featuring the best bits of the two versions. While some elements of the more polished recording were undoubtedly better than the demo, there was a charm and simplicity to the original that seemed to match the emotional vulnerability in Sam's vocal delivery, something deemed vital to the song's overall power. Fitzmaurice even attempted to tidy up slight errors in tempo, including a drum sample Napes had played on the demo, but when corrected, the whole track seemed to lose something and virtually every additional element was eventually discarded again for the final mix.

'The loop wasn't quite right,' Fitzmaurice admitted, 'the timing was slightly off. The other instruments reacted to this, and altogether created something magical that we couldn't get in any other way.' While 'Stay with Me' appears to have had more attention than virtually every other song which would later appear on *In the Lonely Hour*, Fitzmaurice conceded, 'About ninety per cent of it is the demo version.'

As the follow-up single in the UK to 'Money on My Mind', 'Stay with Me' matched that song's success at the end of May 2014 by becoming Sam's second instant No.1 on the UK Singles Chart. As well as being a hit with record buyers, it picked up some rave reviews from online music and entertainment sites, with *Digital Spy* summing up the general opinion. They said, 'As a general rule of thumb, a gospel choir could even make a rendition of last week's shopping list sound powerful, let alone the sensitive musings of a one-night stand. As it swells into an emotional crescendo, [Sam's] soulful voice far outstripping its rousing backing.'

Whatever the song's impact on his home territory, 'Stay with Me' would have international resonance, especially in the US. Released as Sam's first official single there – after a largely unheralded, stop-gap release of the *Nirvana* EP – 'Stay with Me' was nothing short of a phenomenon. While the song never reached No.1 on the Billboard Hot 100, stalling at No.2, it would spend over a year on the chart and has sold almost five million copies to date in the US alone. Around the world, it became a Top-10 hit in over a dozen countries and has proved to be Sam's most successful song to date.

But in the end, that success came at a price. Shortly after 'Stay with Me' started to gain some traction at US radio, picking up spot plays and being added to playlists at stations across the country, the originality of the main melody and the chorus's basic chord structure were called into question. Towards the end of 2014, publishers at Warner/Chappell Music and Sony/ATV Music Publishing, acting on behalf of songwriters Tom Petty and Jeff Lynne, contacted the various music publishers credited with holding the rights to 'Stay with Me', bringing to their attention what they simply described as 'similarities' between the new song and Petty's 'I Won't Back Down'. The latter had been written and recorded by Petty, alongside his co-producer Lynne, for his 1989 album, *Full Moon Fever*. At the time of the request, Sam stated he hadn't even heard Petty's song, maintaining it wasn't a big hit in the UK charts at the time and was therefore rarely played on radio now. He told *CBS News Now*, 'I am twenty-two years old... I've never listened to that song.'

However, in the US, *Full Moon Fever* had been an important milestone in Petty's career, marking his debut as a solo artist, and his first without his regular backing band, The Heartbreakers. The overall sound of the album was heavily influenced by his choice of collaborator for the record, with Petty choosing to work predominantly with Jeff Lynne, the Electric Light Orchestra (ELO) founder. Lynne not only produced the record but shared songwriting credits on over half of the album's twelve tracks, including 'I Won't Back Down', which was chosen as the lead single from the album. As a single, 'I Won't Back Down' would become Petty's biggest US hit in almost a decade, peaking at No.12 on Billboard's Hot 100 and helping *Full Moon Fever* become one of the most successful albums of his career. The album would reach No.3 on the US album charts, spawning a further four singles and was eventually certified 5 x Platinum (for sales in excess of five million copies in the US). While much of the initial success could be attributed to 'I Won't Back Down' and the critical acclaim it received on release, the album's longevity owed more to a third single, 'Free Fallin', which was the album's biggest hit – reaching No.7 on the US Billboard chart – and would prove to be the most enduring song of Petty's long and illustrious career.

While it's true Petty wasn't as commercially successful in the UK, *Full Moon Fever* would provide his undoubted commercial breakthrough in the British charts, delivering his first Top-5 placing on the Official UK Album Chart and 'I Won't Back Down' would prove to be his highest-charting song in the UK when it peaked at No.28 in June 1989. To the casual listener, 'Stay with Me' and 'I Won't Back Down' couldn't be more different, composed twenty-five years apart, and apparently sitting at opposite ends of the musical spectrum. The former, with its emotionally raw vocals, sweeping strings and touches of gospel, could be squarely assigned to the soul-jazz arena, while the latter is firmly rooted in the American tradition of country-rock. But on closer inspection, playing the songs back to back, everyone involved admitted there were elements which could be seen as similar, if not the same.

Sam told *CBS News*, 'It was a complete accident,' before

adding, 'I was very shocked.' While he, Napes and Phillips were willing to accept the two songs did sound alike in some respects, they wanted to make it clear this was nothing more than a freaky coincidence, and there had been no intention to be underhand or deliberately try to copy Petty and Lynne's work. Sam was quick to defend himself and his fellow co-writers by saying, 'It was never a malicious thing,' before concluding, 'It's a very, very regular thing that happens, and I didn't realize that. And I'm still learning all about that stuff.' He and his team did not contest Petty and Lynne's claim, agreeing to their terms, and, as Sam told CBS, 'We [all] tried to deal with it in a very classy way.'

With immediate effect, Petty and Lynne's names were added to the songwriting credits for 'Stay with Me' and subsequently this agreement meant they would receive a twenty-five per cent share (12.5 per cent each) of the song's royalties. In a statement released via his website, Petty stated in a typically wry fashion, 'About the Sam Smith. Let me say I never had any hard feelings toward Sam. All my years of songwriting have shown me these things can happen. Most times you catch it before it gets out the studio door but in this case it got by.' He went on to say, 'Sam did the right thing and I have thought no more about this,' and declared the whole incident, 'a musical accident, no more no less.'
With track sales of 'Stay with Me' approaching five million in the US alone, and the parent album pushing four million worldwide, Petty and Lynne were in line to receive a sizeable, and entirely unexpected, cash windfall.

While the controversy would briefly reignite in early 2015 in the wake of Sam's success at the Grammy Awards, the fact that a couple of extra names had been added to the song's writing credits couldn't undermine the fact that 'Stay with Me' was a standout track from *In the Lonely Hour* and will undoubtedly remain Sam's signature song for some time to come. In the short term, it was about to push *In the Lonely Hour* to multi-platinum status and would eventually propel Sam centre stage at the US's biggest music awards show, the Grammys.

CHAPTER TWELVE

READY
TO FLY

*'I'm very body-conscious. Sometimes I'm really proud that
I don't look like other pop stars. But there's also moments
where I'm like, "Ugh, I wish I had abs like Bieber."'*
Sam Smith on preparing to face the world ahead of his debut
album's release – *Rolling Stone*, January 2015

Towards the end of 2013, with work almost complete on the tracks that would eventually come together as his debut album, Sam began preparing for the year ahead. He'd ended the previous year with a 'One to Watch' interview in the *Guardian*, where he stated, 'Nobody knows who I am. But most of the people in this country have heard me sing.' Behind the scenes, 'Team Sam Smith' was aiming to ensure that Sam would no longer be anonymous.

Clearly, for Sam there would be no going back. While he had managed to live a fairly normal life and maintain a degree of anonymity during much of 2012 and 2013, things were about to change dramatically in the first few months of 2014. Capitol already had comprehensive plans for much of the marketing and media campaign that would accompany the launch of Sam as a solo artist which would neatly lead, towards the middle of the year, with the release of his debut album, *In the Lonely Hour*. However, any plans already made were accelerated somewhat by the announcement that Sam had won two very prestigious music industry awards.

At the beginning of December 2013 Sam had found out he'd been shortlisted for the Brits' Critics' Choice Award and had told BBC News, 'I have watched the Brits religiously for many years growing up. The people who have won before are, to this day, some of my favourite artists and biggest inspirations.' He added, 'To even be up for this award is completely overwhelming for me. I can't begin to tell you how thankful I am.'

Sam wasn't exaggerating. As the British equivalent of the US Grammy Awards, The Brits has become the UK's biggest, and arguably most important, music industry event since its inception in 1977. In 2008, the introduction of the Critics' Choice Award was an attempt to showcase new and upcoming UK talent, with the award open to any artist already signed to a label and expected to release their debut album during the following twelve months. Each year, the eventual winner is selected by votes from a panel of music industry insiders, journalists and tastemakers. In its first year, the honour went to Adele. Her subsequent phenomenal international success went a long way towards giving the award extra weight and its winners undeniable kudos. Since Adele's victory, the award more or less guarantees success for the lucky recipient, with the likes of Florence + the Machine, Jessie J, Emeli Sandé and Ellie Goulding all achieving considerable sales and critical acclaim at home and internationally. Such was the media attention surrounding the award that even a place on the shortlist has been seen as an invaluable launching pad for a fledgling career, with several recent success stories – including Ella Eyre, James Blake and AlunaGeorge – having featured as runners-up in the last few years.

For Sam, it was to be a double celebration, as he was also included on the longlist for the BBC's Sound of 2014 poll and looked likely to place near the top of the final listing. The BBC's list of ones-to-watch had been inauguarated in 2003, growing over the years to become one of the most trusted and influential polls of its type. The longlist, compiled from nominations supplied by over 150 UK music industry experts, DJs, journalists and record producers, was seen as a means of bringing a group of relatively unknown artists to the public's attention. Used to spot exciting, potentially successful new artists, over the years it had played an important role in helping kick-start several fledgling careers. Like the Brits Critics' Choice Award, the BBC Sound of… poll was seen as a reliable guide, pinpointing the bands and artists who were likely to experience their commercial breakthrough in the next year or so, and as such became a useful tool for much of the UK's media and press hoping to be among the first to run features on 'the next big thing'.

In the end, Sam's place as the ultimate 'sure bet' was virtually assured when he not only won the Brit Award, but also beat the likes of Ella Eyre and George Ezra to top the BBC's Sound of 2014 poll. It was hardly a unique achievement: Adele, Jessie J and Ellie Goulding had all taken top honours in previous years, but taking into consideration the international success enjoyed by each of those acts, it was still a relatively elite group and undoubtedly a reassuring indication of what was just around the corner for Sam. Of course, considering the artists who'd won in the past, he was delighted. He told BBC News, 'Even to be a part of it is amazing… It feels incredible.'

But despite Sam fitting the criteria for both awards – with his debut album due in the next six months and never having had a solo Top-20 single – the announcement of his victory did incite a small degree of controversy and a minor backlash against him and the awards. Rock music critic Neil McCormick, in an article published in the *Telegraph*, stated, 'So that's it, apparently. The future has been decided by the great and good of the music industry and all the rest of the young wannabes can go home now. Unless it strikes anyone as odd that an artist being hailed as the next big thing has already scored a massive number-one single.' Pointing to Sam's previous involvement with Disclosure and, in particular, Naughty Boy, McCormick may have had a point but in real terms, Sam's route to success was fast becoming the norm for countless new artists, and the Brits and BBC polls were merely reflecting that evolution and marking it as a valid means of entry into the music industry.

Any worries Sam might have had about being thought of as a faceless voice on other people's records were evaporating swiftly as he started to concentrate on promoting his own career rather than the artists he'd previously worked with. He told *Pigeons and Planes*, 'These awards give it this beautiful platform. It kind of projects your face and you to the whole of the UK so it's mad. But I don't feel pressure because I have too much belief in my work.'

For him, just being associated with both awards was a huge boost to his profile. Actually winning acted as the perfect launch pad for the album's introductory single, 'Money on My Mind', and gave him a forum to talk about his forthcoming debut album. Sam was in a fortunate position, in that all the songs for *In the Lonely Hour* had been recorded and the album was all but complete. While many might have crumbled under the weight of expectation or strained to cope with the added scrutiny, he was taking it all in his stride, telling *The Line of Best Fit*, 'I have this album that I'm proud of and worked so hard on… all I am is excited,' before adding, 'I would definitely feel the pressure if – one, my album wasn't finished, because I would have to finish it. And second of all, I would definitely feel the pressure if the hype around me was not my music and was about my personal life and not related to art.'

In retrospect, it seems a little naive of him to think the music he was making would be the only thing people were interested in during the run-up to the release of the album. Over the course of the next few months, he would feel the full glare of the media spotlight and in the process he'd have to confront some uncomfortable truths about fame and life in the public eye.

It's a sad fact that the music press in general, and much of the wider media specifically, feel the need to pigeon-hole new artists almost as soon as they appear, desperate to apply genre labels or immediately find easy, some might say lazy, comparisons with other artists. Sam was no exception. First and foremost was the obvious connections made between Sam and previous Brit and BBC's Sound Of… winner, Adele.

For much of 2014, Adele's name would be inextricably linked with Sam's in countless articles and reviews, with reference to everything from musical similarities to physical appearance. With many publications and websites desperate to make a point, there were endless lists of co-writers, musicians, recording studios and career milestones, which the pair had in common. Sam had been a fan of Adele's from the very beginning of her career and, in some respects, he was flattered by the association, telling *Pigeons and Planes*, 'Obviously Adele is just unbelievable,' before admitting, 'I'm just more intrigued to meet her, she seems like the loveliest girl in the world... I'd love to just get in a room with her and pick her brain.' But, talking to *Rolling Stone*, he was concerned the media's hunger to find 'The New Adele', while simultaneously desperate to label him as soon as he appeared on the scene was mistakenly linking them. 'We're very different,' he insisted. 'I feel like the constant comparisons might piss her off. It just annoys me that people can't digest two pop stars singing really personal songs, who don't look like normal pop stars.' But in terms of more direct similarities, he was quick to confront the issue head-on, stating in *P&P*, 'I really want to stay away from the comparisons between me and her because I think it's just easy to put people in boxes and compare. I mean, there are similarities, I can see that, but we're also very different people with very different stories.' He would be slightly more forthright, but similarly diplomatic when he later told *Billboard*, 'I ultimately think our music's completely different, but if I'm going to be compared to anyone, it's amazing.'

Putting aside any similarities between their musical styles

or lyrical content, what Adele's success had actually done for Sam was far more radical and signalled an important shift in the music industry's approach to marketing new artists, especially those who didn't necessarily conform to what was deemed an appropriate 'look'. If Adele's impressive sales around the world had proved one thing, it was that musicians and, perhaps more significantly, female artists, no longer had to conform to a certain body type or image. For Sam, as someone who had previously experienced criticism about his weight, it was a welcome change. He told *Fader*, 'I've had some horrible things said to me in my life, so I'm quite immune to things like that.' But immune or not, he was keen for any stigma about size and shape to become irrelevant. He continued, 'I do care about the way I look,' before concluding, 'I can see why people would go crazy… But I don't give a shit. I just need to have the best body I can and feel confident in that.' Talking to *Mclean's*, he was even more direct, saying, 'I'm very proud that I don't look like a pop star. I don't want to.'

During the final run-up to the release of his record, Sam had come to realise exactly what kind of music he wanted to present to the public. He had endeavoured to stay true to what he felt was an honest representation of who he was and what he wanted his songs to say and he didn't want to undermine it all by falling at the final hurdle. He told *Vibe*, 'I think if we're going to talk about the percentage of people who are ripped, and skinny and beautiful-looking, we're not all like that.' He continued, 'I will take a page out of Adele's book. She said, "I make music for the ears, not the eyes." I will say that too. I make music for people to listen to – for people to hear my voice and hear what I'm saying. I'm not bothered about what I'm wearing or my weight.'

But Sam was smart enough to know everyone didn't think the same way he did and he was ready to face the inevitable scrutiny. He told *Digital Spy*, 'As I've got into the industry I've realised how important it is to keep in control of the music you're putting out and the way you're presented because it's vicious out there.' If his assertion that his songs were a glimpse of the real person singing them then he wanted the image he presented to be just as genuine: 'I just wanna be real and I want to come across just like me, normal. I'm not afraid to put myself out there – in all senses of the word.' He went on: 'We all know the type of artist I want to be, and I don't wanna be that guy who people care more about what I'm wearing to the coffee shop than my next single. I don't wanna be that guy.'

But the kind of guy Sam did want to be was clear: he wanted his music to do the talking. He felt he was simply adding to the diversity that needed to exist in the music industry. He told the *Telegraph*, 'There should be artists out there of all different shapes, sizes, colours and sexualities.' But most of all what he wanted was his image to remain a secondary concern. Sam was adamant that how he looked would never outshine the music or, perhaps more importantly, distract from his voice. 'It's my voice that's the instrument,' he told *Fader*. 'What I'm trying to do with my album is show that it's my voice that's leading.'

With this in mind he decided the image he presented to the public would be enduring and uncomplicated. As a specific look, it would perhaps be best exemplified by the photograph which would later feature on the cover of the *In the Lonely Hour* album – a rather pensive-looking Sam, hands clenched in front of his face as if in prayer, dressed entirely in black. Sam explained *to Mclean's*, 'I want to bring class into mainstream pop. I want that timelessness back. It just makes sense when you sing soul. When Frank Sinatra was twenty years old, he was in a suit. So I want to be in one too.'

Thus, from the launch period of *In the Lonely Hour* and beyond, Sam has rarely been seen in anything other than simple, monochrome shirts and jackets or his trusted, well-tailored suits. As he would soon find out, with success comes status. Now, with many of the world's top designers and labels, including Calvin Klein, Casely-Hayford and Armani, providing the majority of his wardrobe, Sam's image has evolved and, whether setting foot on the red carpet or on stage at an awards show, he does so with an undeniable air of sophistication and class.

Similarly, Sam had decided he didn't want to add any form of dance moves or choreography to his stage shows. He explained to *Vibe*, 'The music industry has gotten to a place where there aren't many artists who stand and sing and play, which is what they're supposed to be doing.' Sam said he found it increasingly distracting when his peers seemed more intent on performing a dance routine flawlessly than delivering a perfect vocal. He told the *Telegraph*, 'It's quite frustrating actually when you do shows and you're the only person not twerking. I get angry, like, "Why am I the only one standing there singing?" People should be doing that.'

While his own media and public image and his growing

self-confidence were factors he would have complete control over, Sam would soon be forced to face a decidedly more unpredictable aspect of losing the anonymity he'd so far enjoyed. He had become increasingly aware of the intrusion and unwanted attention that often goes hand-in-hand with success. As someone who was sometimes a little too keen to share his innermost thoughts and with a tendency to be overly candid, there were obvious pitfalls to be avoided. As with most people who are thrust into the public eye, the other element of Sam's personal life sure to come under the media's microscope was his sexuality. As he was already 'out' to his family, close friends and his professional inner circle, he seemed equally adamant to remain forthright and as open as possible to his fans, as well as with the media at large, on that particular subject.

Over the last couple of decades, while several other pop stars have either attempted to keep their sexuality ambiguous, or have decided to 'come out' after they've already achieved a certain amount of success or critical recognition for their music, Sam's situation was relatively unique. He was an openly gay man at the very start of his career. Even in terms of promoting his work, he had never shied away from the subject of being gay, given that some of his earliest interviews were conducted with gay websites and magazines. So unlike Boy George who had coyly stated he preferred 'a cup of tea to sex', or George Michael, whose career in America had more or less crumbled overnight following his very public 'outing' in 1998, Sam's sexuality was sure to be a topic of interest from the outset.

But secure as Sam was, he had no interest in becoming

a spokesman for the gay community or having his music sidelined or viewed as something rather niche. As far as he was concerned, he didn't make 'gay music'. Former Bronski Beat and Communards' vocalist Jimmy Somerville had always been extremely vocal about his own sexuality, with his songs projecting a very clear and often fairly political message. And while it hadn't prevented him from achieving a certain degree of success for either of his bands, or as a solo artist, Somerville often found himself marginalised. Dismissed as merely being a 'gay artist', whose audience was predominantly gay and therefore whose music was expected to conform to certain stereotypes, he had sometimes struggled to be respected as an artist with universal appeal.

This was a trap Sam was determined to avoid completely. He told *Fader*, 'I am comfortable with myself and my life is amazing in that respect. I've been treated as normal as anyone in my life; I've had no issues. I do know that some people have issues in life, but I haven't, and it's as normal as my right arm. I want to make it a normality because this is a non-issue.' He went on to say, 'People put things in boxes; it makes it easier to digest information. Why is [my sexuality] a talking point? I'm singing, I'm making music, I'm performing music – that's what should be the talking point.'

From the outset, Sam had made it very clear in interviews the subject of the majority of the songs on his album was unrequited love, and in particular, his unrequited love for a man who had turned out to be straight. But he was adamant the sex of the protagonists and the objects of their affections in his songs were irrelevant: it was the emotions expressed in his songs, and the universality of the feelings behind them, which were far more interesting, and thus, more important for him to project successfully. And perhaps more significantly, he wanted them to reach as wide an audience as possible. He revealed: 'I've tried to be clever with this album, because it's also important to me that my music reaches everybody. I've made my music so that it could be about anything and everybody – whether it's a guy, a female or a goat – and everybody can relate to that. I'm not in this industry to talk about my personal life unless it's in a musical form.'

It would seem Sam was setting out his stall very early. He was ready to take the prying and extra scrutiny which inevitably accompanied life in the public eye, but he was also determined it would never inhibit what he wanted to say in his songs, or overshadow his music in any way. As far as he was concerned he had made an album of deeply personal, confessional love songs that just happened to be about another man. He was never going to hide his true sexuality or try to lie about it, but he was equally determined it was not something he wanted to define him or have any influence in shaping his future as an artist. While his stance caused a degree of controversy and a minor backlash among some gay magazines and websites, his determination to stick to his principles was based on his need to make up his own mind and make his own mistakes. As he told *Mclean's*, when asked if he felt he'd put extra pressure on himself by being openly gay, Sam said, 'I don't know yet... I'm still figuring that out for myself.'

About to release his debut album, Sam was understandably nervous about the effect fame might have on his life as a whole, but, as he told *Fader*, he had learned a certain something about stubbornness and sticking to what he believed in from his mother and her experiences. 'I do worry about it,' he confessed. 'But I also have a very strong head on my shoulders and I'm not willing to be someone I'm not for the sake of other people.'

As the UK release date for *In the Lonely Hour* approached, there was still one fairly important piece of unfinished business for Sam to deal with. It had become abundantly clear, after the instant and widespread success of 'Money on My Mind' and then 'Stay with Me', that the album was likely to make quite a splash on its initial release. Media interest in Sam was already surpassing his and his team's initial expectations. Under this type of media spotlight, there was no doubt the subject matter of the album's key songs was going to raise some awkward questions for Sam. With this in mind, he had decided he needed to tell the man who'd broken his heart the truth, confess the depth of his feelings towards him and explain that he had in fact inspired most of the songs featured on *In the Lonely Hour*.

CHAPTER THIRTEEN

TAKING ON
THE WORLD

'I'm just really proud of putting out something so personal.
I just hope people get that and listen to it and understand
how much I put out there on the line.'
Sam Smith on releasing his debut album,
In the Lonely Hour – The Line of Best Fit, February 2014

I t wasn't until early February 2015, following Sam's
appearance at the Grammy Awards, that widespread
press speculation about the man he had thanked in his
acceptance speech prompted countless newspapers,
magazines and entertainment websites to claim they had
solved the mystery surrounding the man who had broken
Sam's heart. And while Sam himself has never revealed the
identity of the man he credits with inspiring him to write
the unrequited love songs which form the heart of the *In
the Lonely Hour* album, some media reports speculated
that it was Elvin Smith, the manager who helped shape the
most recent chapter of his career.

It's clear the pair had formed a close friendship and natural
working relationship over the years. Sam often credits Elvin
with restoring some of the confidence he'd lost during the

years he struggled to be heard and without him it's unlikely he would have met Jimmy Napes, the Disclosure twins or Naughty Boy. Elvin is straight and happily married. Over time it reports speculated that Sam's feelings towards him had developed beyond mere friendship, or even a passing crush, turning into something much deeper and more difficult to ignore. But as Sam has stated on numerous occasions, rather than talking to the unidentified man himself, he would pour his heart out during writing and recording sessions with close friends like Jimmy Napes (as well as relative strangers such as Eg White and Fraser T. Smith) and sought comfort within the lyrics they were creating together. But as the album neared completion and Sam realised how much attention the lyrical content of the songs might generate, he decided the best thing to do was to come clean, tell the man involved and perhaps he'd get some closure along the way. Sam would eventually tell *The Sun* newspaper, 'I was the only one in the relationship. It was in my mind and was something I had to get over.' He went on to clarify, 'He's not gay. Nothing ever happened between us. I know he loved me too, but not in that way.'

Talking to the *Guardian*, Sam explained how the whole process of making the album had forced him to examine elements of his personal life more thoroughly and pulled recent events into sharper focus. He said, 'When I fell in love with this guy last year, it was the third person in my life I had had really strong feelings for and they'd never loved me back. And this album was almost a way for me to break the cycle. I will never let myself fall in love with someone again in that way.' He went on to explain that finishing the record had brought him relief and catharsis and he was ready to move on to a new chapter in his life. In an interview with *The Sun*, Sam said, 'I feel nothing towards him now. I'll always love him but I'm not in love with him anymore. I definitely don't crease on the floor in pain anymore... I also made the record so that this doesn't happen again. I don't want to fall in love again with someone who doesn't love me back.'

In retrospect, it seems like Sam was finally taking back control of his own life and he was just doing what needed to be done, but at the time he was understandably nervous and uncertain about how things would play out. Without ever identifying the man, he explained to the *Guardian* exactly when and how he'd finally revealed the truth. Sam admitted, 'I told him a week before the album came out. He'd heard the record, but didn't have a clue it was about him. He just said, "Are you ok?" It was a lovely response.'

Sam was undoubtedly in a healthier frame of mind about everything by the time he'd started doing promotion for *In the Lonely Hour*. He'd accepted the reality of the situation and was trying to work through it calmly and in a mature fashion, but it seems he wasn't afraid to use the promo circuit as a means of finding even greater comfort. He told *Fader*, 'Obviously it was never going to go the way I wanted it to go, but it was good as a form of closure, to get it off my chest and tell him. I feel better for it. I feel almost like I signed off this part of my life where I keep giving myself to guys who are never going to love me back. He welcomed the chance to talk about it: 'It feels good to have interviews like this, to chat about it and put stuff to bed. It's all there now, and I can move on and hopefully find a guy who can love me the way I love him.'

When *In the Lonely Hour* was released in the UK on 26 May 2014, exactly one week after his twenty-first birthday, Sam was feeling slightly overwhelmed by the way everything seemed to have snowballed and, in what felt like the blink of an eye, how much his life had changed. Only a couple of months earlier, he had completed his biggest UK shows to date and his first string of American concerts, covering key cities throughout the country and across the border into Canada, had been a resounding success. He now had two solo number one singles under his belt and within hours of its release *In the Lonely Hour* was already No.1 on the iTunes album chart. The following Sunday, it was announced the album had entered the Official UK Album Chart in pole position, with sales in excess of 102,000 copies, becoming the fastest-selling debut album of the year.

During its first year on release, *In the Lonely Hour* spawned a further three Top-10 singles and enjoyed an extraordinary unbroken chart run inside the UK Top 10, only dropping out of the Top 5 for two weeks and actually climbing all the way to the number one spot on six separate occasions. That unbroken run inside the UK Album Chart Top 5 almost surpassed a chart record established by The Beatles' first album, 1963's *Please Please Me*.

In the official 2014 year-end round-up, *In the Lonely Hour* was named the second best-selling album of the year, behind Ed Sheeran's sophomore release, *X*, but it was named the biggest-selling debut, with the OCC website reporting sales in excess of 1.25 million copies. In what had turned out to be an exceptional year for British artists, who occupied the entire Top 10 of the year-end chart for the first time since sales records began, it was a particularly sweet victory for Sam. The success he'd enjoyed in his home country was replicated internationally, with *In the Lonely Hour* reaching the Top 20 in over twenty-five countries around the world. But perhaps his greatest achievement so far was his incredible breakthrough in the United States.

While success in the UK can go a long way towards opening doors and creating a buzz across the Atlantic, it's by no means a guarantee of success. If you need proof, just ask Robbie Williams. During his time as a member of Take That, one of the UK's most successful boy bands, Williams became a household name. After quitting the group in 1995, his solo career started on shaky ground, with his first album, *Life Thru a Lens*, debuting outside the Top 10 and the album's first three singles enjoyed a steep downward spiral in terms of their peak chart positions. Towards the end of 1997 his fortunes were somewhat reversed by the release of 'Angels' and he has gone on to become one of the UK's biggest-selling home-grown acts, with eleven UK No.1 albums, twenty-nine Top-10 singles and multiple sell-out arena tours and stadium dates. But in the US, Robbie's career is virtually non-existent. Save for Take That's 'Back For Good', which climbed all the way to No.7 on the Billboard Hot 100 singles chart, he has so far failed to crack either the US albums or singles Top 40 as a solo artist. Things may have changed in terms of UK artists being given greater opportunities to reach the US audience they deserve, with the success of artists such as Adele and Ed Sheeran going a long way towards signalling a more even playing field, but even in this context, Sam's achievement was still fairly extraordinary.

In the Lonely Hour was eventually released in the States towards the end of June 2014, a month later than in the UK. It arrived less than fifteen months after Sam had played to his very first American audience – at the Coachella Valley Music and Arts Annual Festival alongside Disclosure. When the album entered the Billboard Top 200 Album chart at No.2, just behind Lana Del Rey's second album, *Ultraviolence*, having sold over 166,000 copies, it sealed Sam's status as the UK's hottest new export. In the process it became the fastest-selling debut album by a British male artist, beating the opening week tally of Ed Sheeran's debut, +, by more than 100,000 sales and dwarfing the 6,300 sales Adele's *19* album achieved during its first week on sale, back in June 2008. The US breakthrough showed all the signs of being a perfectly timed, well-orchestrated effort on behalf of Sam, his management and the team at Capitol, but in reality it was yet another example of the type of lucky break which had increasingly played a part in his recent successes.

Sam's assault on the American market really began in late 2013, with a couple of sell-out shows at one of Los Angeles' most prestigious concert venues, The Troubadour. Despite having a capacity of less than 500, The Troubadour has become synonymous with launching the US careers of some of the world's most revered artists and songwriters, including Elton John, Joni Mitchell and Van Morrison. It was undoubtedly the type of showcase Capitol hoped would open some doors with US TV and radio stations and their initial faith in Sam was handsomely rewarded.

Within a couple of months he was booked to appear as the musical guest on the long-running US comedy show,

Saturday Night Live, bucking the show's trend of featuring only predominately established acts. When Sam took to the *SNL* stage on 29 March 2014, he not only became one of just a handful of brand new artists to ever appear on the show, but he did so with no current single to promote and three months ahead of his debut album. He looked back on that night in an interview with *Entertainment Weekly*: '*Saturday Night Live* was one of the scariest nights of my entire life,' he admitted. 'I tried to beg my managers and my team to not do *SNL* because I thought it was way too early.' While he may have had a point, there was very little sign of hesitation on display when he took his cue from the show's guest host, comedian Louis CK, and stepped up to the microphone. He gave a stunning live performance of 'Stay with Me', followed later in the show by a similarly arresting version of 'Lay Me Down', to the small crowd in the room and the considerably larger television audience watching in homes across America.

The next day, *Rolling Stone* reviewed his appearance under the headline, 'Sam Smith dazzles in *SNL* debut', before reporting, '[For "Stay with Me"] Sam Smith brought out a gospel choir to support him though the arrangement left enough room for his buttery vocals to take center stage.' They were similarly impressed with his performance of 'Lay Me Down', saying, 'Smith showed off what he can do standing largely on his own, with little more than spare keys and a cello accompanying him.'

Sam was the first to admit he had underestimated the audience's willingness to accept someone as relatively untested as he was, telling *EW*, 'I was so, so wrong. It was incredible and it's broken me in America.' For him, it wasn't merely the fact the gamble seemed to be paying off despite a nagging voice in his head telling him he was breaking some unwritten code about how British acts were supposed to break America, it was also the incredible speed at which it was happening. He said, 'I'm very aware of the kind of order and the kind of rules in place with people who come from the UK. What we were doing on *SNL* defied all of that. No one knew who I was. He continued, 'That night, people were recognizing me a bit more. It was hours after, actually. You could feel the shift and you could feel the change physically in that moment in New York and it was amazing. It was really surreal.'

The real impact of his *SNL* performance would only be felt a couple of weeks later, in mid-April 2014, when 'Stay with Me' was finally released as Sam's official US debut single. In the wake of the press and media coverage he had enjoyed immediately after the *SNL* transmission, 'Stay With Me' started a steady climb up the Billboard Hot 100, eventually peaking at No.2 and racking up sales to date in the region of 5 million copies. In terms of Sam's US launch, it had effectively accelerated the whole process by several months, moving it more or less in sync with the UK release of the album, and ensuring there was no longer any doubt about who Sam Smith was when *In the Lonely Hour* was released a couple of months later.

Reflecting on recent events in September 2014, Sam told *Digital Spy*, 'The whole American thing completely wasn't planned. I can't explain how unplanned it was.' Elaborating further, he admitted, 'I've intensely watched the industry and watched how it all works with English artists. I'm breaking at the same time – it's really odd.' Noting the fact that *In the Lonely Hour* had actually sold more in its first week in the US than it did in the UK, Sam stated, 'My numbers in America are higher than my numbers here. Obviously it's a bigger country, but it's really surreal for it to be happening in this order.'

Sam's observation wasn't too far off the mark, and while his simultaneous success on both sides of the Atlantic wasn't unprecedented, it was fairly unusual for any artist from outside America to see their debut album released in the US without a longer promotional lead-in and considerably more exposure in the media. While Ed Sheeran released his debut album, +, in the UK in September 2011 to instant acclaim and commercial success, it wasn't until June 2012, a full nine months later, when the album finally received a release in the US and even Adele had to wait six months between the UK and US release for her debut, *19*.

In more recent times, release dates are often staggered to accommodate touring schedules and the availability of the artists for promotional appearances across several different territories. It was this type of release pattern which saw the self-titled debut from Australian boy band, 5 Seconds of Summer, released over several different dates in different countries, arriving in the US a full month after it had charted in their home country and the UK. This type of release schedule allows the artist sufficient time to concentrate fully on each territory, either by touring there or being available for media and press during the run-up to release.

Sam was worried that by releasing *In the Lonely Hour* more

or less simultaneously around the world, he would be forced to spend too much time in the US, and thus would ignore other territories including his own country. He told *Digital Spy*, 'I was worrying I was spending too much time in the US, because UK people get sick of people who spend too much time there. It's really hard to balance out what you're doing.' He then admitted, 'I had a panic attack the other day. I was thinking, "F*ck. The UK is so important to me. It's everything – it's my home. I love America but it's important for me to be [in the UK] and be an artist and be well known here."'

In real terms, he had little to worry about. Sam was (and still is) very active across social media platforms, including Twitter, Facebook and Instagram, and his UK fans seemed content enough simply to use these methods to stay in touch with him when he couldn't actually be in the country himself. Thus, for much of the second half of 2014, he was jetting back and forward to the US, as well as performing up and down the UK and across Europe.

The time Sam spent promoting his record in America was paying dividends. He was not only reaping the rewards in terms of continued commercial success but also enjoying widespread critical acclaim, and picking up a few celebrity fans along the way. It was hard to keep up with his hectic work and social life during this period and his new-found celebrity status meant it became virtually impossible to avoid his countless selfies alongside Taylor Swift, Katy Perry and Rihanna. Sam was wholeheartedly welcomed into the inner circles of countless US recording artists and celebrities, and it was obvious he was overjoyed at such an outpouring of love and respect from his peers.

As his album continued to sell on both sides of the Atlantic, Sam kept things moving in the different territories by releasing singles and remixes which catered directly to these individual markets. In the UK, 'Lay Me Down' was re-recorded as a duet with John Legend, sending the song to No.1 and raising money for the Comic Relief charity, while in the US, respected R&B producer Rodney Jerkins remixed 'Stay with Me' to make it more accessible to the American market.

Jerkins' career stretches back to the mid-1990s, where he first found success writing and producing for the likes of Destiny's Child, Brandy and Toni Braxton. Over the next couple of decades, he worked alongside some of the biggest names in pop music, including Michael Jackson, Beyoncé and Lady Gaga. Working under the name 'Darkchild', Jerkins remixed 'Stay with Me' and subsequently turned his remix into a duet between Sam and Mary J. Blige. Both of these versions proved enormously popular with Sam's US fans, turning the song into a radio phenomenon and subsequently leading to the Darkchild version picking up nominations, and eventually the actual awards, for Song of the Year and Record of the Year at the 2015 Grammy Awards.

Selling over a million copies of his album in America was probably enough of a reward for Sam – it confirmed everything he'd been working for in the previous decade or so – but in the US true validation comes in the shape of recognition at the annual Grammy Awards. While his commercial success in the US was undeniable, his status as *the* breakout artist of the year would be set in stone when he received a total of six nominations, including nods for Best

New Artist and Album of the Year. Before the nominations had even been announced, Sam found himself at the centre of countless speculative conversations with journalists and interviewers, but he was keen to play down any talk of him picking up multiple nominations or being that year's 'dark horse' in the race. He told *Vibe*, 'I don't even want to talk about it too much because I don't want to jinx anything but if that happened that would be unbelievable. Being nominated for anything is truly incredible.' As a life-long follower of the Grammys, he was well aware how important they were to any artist, both in terms of sales and credibility, and he wasn't taking the chance of victory in any category lightly.

On the day the nominations were announced, Sam was enjoying a rare day off ahead of performing at the Staples Center in Los Angeles that evening. With so many categories to get through, the nomination announcements took an exceptionally long time and he ended up spending much of the day in his hotel room surrounded by his team, waiting for the full list to be revealed. Several hours later, on finally being told he'd received a total of six nominations, Sam admitted to BBC News, 'It's been the most weirdly emotional day... I'm emotionally drained,' before saying, 'It's a complete dream come true... I wasn't expecting it.' Expressing his complete surprise while sharing the good news with his fans via Twitter, Sam exclaimed, 'What is going on!! 6 Grammy nominations. Dear Lord.'

He was obviously overjoyed to receive such esteemed recognition so soon after breaking America and there was no denying it was quite an achievement. In fact he had received more nominations than considerably more established acts such as Beyoncé, Ed Sheeran, Taylor Swift and Pharrell Williams – and all within six months of releasing his debut album. Sam was giddy at the prospect of winning just one award, but as always he was determined to stress he wouldn't let it change who he was inside if he did succeed. In an interview with *Mclean's*, he confided, 'It will make me proud. But I'll always be unconfident. I think that's a good thing because my insecurity is what I write about. You never know what will happen, though. It would be incredible if I could just get one.' Finally, he quipped, 'I hope it doesn't make me too big-headed – that won't be good for business.' When one fan asked Sam how he planned to celebrate if he won, he joked, via his Facebook page, 'I'll strip,' before swiftly adding, 'No, no, I won't do that.'

But it seems it wasn't the thought of not winning which was troubling Sam most. Instead he appeared to be more concerned about going head-to-head against his beloved Beyoncé! Sam made it very clear he felt Beyoncé would be a worthy winner on the night and he'd happily concede defeat, telling *Mclean's*, 'It will be truly understandable if Beyoncé goes away with everything.' Beyoncé's self-titled album was a personal favourite of Sam's and he had already stated he not only felt the songs on the record were some of her best, but the whole release strategy and marketing surrounding the album had been groundbreaking and revolutionary. He told *Rolling Stone*, 'She deserves it way more than I do. I'd be embarrassed if I got it over her. If I got it, I'd give it to her.' While it's doubtful Sam's management and record label were feeling quite so generous, it's clear everyone in his

SAM SMITH

corner was preparing for an exciting and eventful evening on 8 February.

The evening got off to a great start for Sam. He'd barely had time to find his seat – conveniently quite near the Staples Center stage – when he was announced as the winner of the Best New Artist award, presented, rather fittingly, by Sam's new BFF, Taylor Swift. Visibly shocked and obviously delighted, Sam said, 'Oh, my gosh... I've got to try and say something now without crying,' before desperately trying to remember his 'thank you' list. His speech ended with a shout-out to his family, as he exclaimed, 'Mum and Dad, Lily and Mabel! I won a Grammy.' There would be an emotional family reunion backstage after the show, with Sam's sister, Mabel, tweeting about her brother's big win the next day: 'Feeling so lucky to be able to witness last night, so insanely proud of him! What an overwhelming night.'

Aside from winning his first Grammy, one of the other highlights of the evening was the chance to perform 'Stay with Me' as a duet with Mary J. Blige and recreate the re-recorded version live on stage. It was a breathtaking performance by anyone's standards and truly showcased Sam at his most confident and assured. There can't be many twenty-two-year-old artists willing to go toe-to-toe with such an accomplished and highly regarded vocalist as Blige, especially singing live, on what was essentially their debut US single and in front of the star-studded Grammy audience.

As the night progressed, Sam made three more trips to the stage, collecting the awards for Best Pop Vocal Album for *In the Lonely Hour*, and then Song of the Year and Record of the Year for the Darkchild remix of 'Stay with Me'.

His acceptance speech for the first of these three awards was probably his most heartfelt and reflective. Revealing the many sacrifices he'd willingly made over the years, he highlighted the enormous pressure exerted on most new artists to conform, to look or sound a certain way, and he emphasised how his rejection of such restrictions shaped what could essentially be viewed as his personal mission statement and had eventually become a rallying cry to his fans. Sam said, 'I just want to say that before I made this record I was doing everything to try and get my music heard. I tried to lose weight and I was making awful music and it was only when I started to be myself that the music started to flow and people started to listen.' He ended with the words, 'So thank you guys for accepting me for just being me. Thank you.'

It was during the speeches he made later in the evening, picking up the awards for 'Stay with Me', when Sam acknowledged the people who had directly influenced the whole of the *In the Lonely Hour* project. Firstly, on accepting the Song of the Year award, he stated, 'I'm having a really, really, really good night,' before introducing Jimmy Napes as 'my therapist for a year.' Secondly, perhaps more poignantly, and definitely with a knowing smile, Sam thanked the 'mystery man' who'd inspired him to write most of the songs on *In the Lonely Hour*, saying, 'I wanna thank the man who this record is about, who I fell in love with last year. Thank you so much for breaking my heart because you got me four Grammys.' It was part 'kiss-off', part affectionate taunt, but it certainly hit the right note with the audience on the night, and helped fuel a great deal of press and media speculation on the subject in the days and weeks which followed.

While Sam was staying tight-lipped about his 'inspiration', countless websites, newspapers and magazines continued to speculate that Elvin Smith was Sam's unrequited love and pictures of the pair celebrating, alongside the rest of Sam's team, filled the front pages and website photo galleries for weeks. When asked by *Rolling Stone* if the mysterious subject of his hit album would get to see his Grammys, Sam admitted, 'I'll be seeing him soon,' before joking, 'So I can let him touch the Grammy – once.' As far as he was concerned his 'mystery man' would remain just that – a mystery.

Ahead of his big Grammy win, Sam told *Entertainment Tonight* he didn't want to think about winning or losing, insisting he saw the whole experience as the icing on an already delicious cake. He said, 'I'm just trying to enjoy the moment. To me this is a celebration of an amazing year and a half so that's how I'm trying to think of it.' And after his multiple Grammy haul, it would seem his feelings hadn't changed. Winning four Grammy awards could be seen as a fitting end to any artist's journey to find acceptance and commercial success, but for Sam, still at the earliest stages of his career, it was merely the close of the first chapter.

CHAPTER FOURTEEN

TRANSFORMATION

'I couldn't bring out In the Lonely Hour and go to the
Grammys with someone. I had to be lonely for the Grammys.'
Sam Smith on walking the red carpet alone on his
big night – *Hello! Magazine*, February 2015

By anyone's standards, 2014 had been a remarkable year for Sam professionally. He'd finished recording his debut album, *In the Lonely Hour*, which on release had been an enormous hit virtually everywhere in the world. He'd toured the globe, singing his songs for thousands of adoring fans every night in sell-out arenas and stadiums and ended the year with the announcement of his six Grammy nominations.

However, as far as his personal life was concerned, 2013, and much of 2014, had been considerably less rewarding. While much of the rejection and heartbreak he experienced during this period had filtered into the songs he was writing for his record, and had therefore played an important role in its eventual success, Sam was ready to close the door on that particular aspect of his life once and for all and move on.

Towards the end of 2014, he met someone who was both gay and available, and it would seem he'd finally fallen for someone who was more than willing to 'love him back'. Sam considered himself to be old fashioned when it came to relationships. Already he had spoken about his personal aversion to one-night stands, casual sex and more modern trends, such as the use of 'dating apps'. He obviously wanted to meet someone, get to know them and then fall in love – old school. Sam confessed to *Rolling Stone*, 'I'm a romantic,' before elaborating, 'I feel like with Grindr and Tinder, you just lose a bit of romance. You're swiping someone's face to the left. The guys I've fallen in love with aren't the most beautiful people you've ever seen. I would've swiped them.' It's safe to say there was very little swiping going on when Sam met a certain, very attractive model/dancer towards the end of 2014.

Sam met Jonathan Zeizel during the weeks running up to Christmas 2014 and the pair seemed to hit it off even more while filming the promo video for Sam's 'Like I Can' single in New York. The black-and-white, Sophie Muller-directed clip shows Sam and a large group of tuxedo-clad men (including Zeizel) at night on the streets of New York, hitting bars, climbing fire escapes and dancing in alleyways. In terms of what the song meant to Sam, it was a fairly momentous occasion. At that moment at least, 'Like I Can' was intended to be the final single to be lifted from his album and, in many ways, filming the video signalled 'closure' for the entire *In the Lonely Hour* project.

On 23 December, Sam took to Twitter to announce, 'Just wrapped up my last music video for this album & my last work thing before Christmas & my holiday. I feel like a kid before summer haha.' It would seem he smuggled a special gift for himself away from the video set! Zeizel, apparently based in New York, had obviously caught his eye, but it appears he wasn't the only potential love interest in Sam's life at that particular moment. Towards the end of November, in an interview with GQ, Sam explained how he had started to imagine finally finding someone he could fall in love with, but how he was still attracted to men who seemed tantalisingly just out of reach. He confessed, 'I feel so much more comfortable wanting what I'm never going to get... I want something that's unobtainable.' Sam went on to say, 'Like recently, I met two guys. One of them on paper is perfect and ticks all the boxes. The other is dangerous and – well, he ticks boxes actually, too.' Sam considered Zeizel to be the one he wanted to do some 'box ticking' with. 'I've chosen him. I want that excitement,' he continued. Indeed he appeared to be instantly smitten, telling *Rolling Stone*, 'He's amazing. A really kind guy, and he's very talented. He's the most amazing dancer.'

Pictures taken at Taylor Swift's twenty-fifth birthday party in early December, showing Sam and Jonathan together, looking happy (if a little worse for wear), were posted on the pair's separate Instagram accounts and it would seem Sam was keen to make their relationship public, even if Zeizel wasn't quite up to speed with what was going on. After only a few weeks, Sam told *The Sun*, 'It's very early days. I'm talking very, very, very early days. But he's really sweet,' and added, 'It's a surreal thing to be talking about because I haven't even confirmed with him that we're officially seeing each other. He'll probably hear about this now.'

'Official' or not, Sam decided Zeizel would be the perfect holiday companion for his forthcoming trip to Australia. Sam intended to spend New Year in Sydney, taking a well-earned break prior to the start of his upcoming US tour, which was due to kick off in Atlanta on 9 January 2015. Judging by the photos uploaded to their Instagram pages over the next couple of weeks – which showed the couple sightseeing in Sydney Harbour, dining out with Australian pop star Ricki-Lee Coulter and relaxing at the beach – Sam had indeed found a suitable match. Finally he was getting the chance to let his hair down and there were reports of drinking and dancing sessions which went on into the early hours and even a bit of late night skinny-dipping. Perhaps it's just as well the pair were sensible enough to refrain from posting any photographic evidence of that particular evening on Instagram, but Sam admitted to *Rolling Stone* they hadn't really thought everything through: 'Afterwards, we were like, "Maybe we shouldn't have done that, because there's sharks".'

But just in case Sam's fans were worried he was enjoying himself too much and his newfound contentment might affect the subject matter and tone for any forthcoming music projects, Sam told *The Sun*, 'People need to realise I'm never going to be happy. The reason I do what I do is because I'm an artist who is always going to be blue about something.'

It would appear Sam was about to see his prediction come true sooner than he'd hoped. By the middle of January, only a couple of weeks into the US dates, his press team at Capitol confirmed Sam was no longer dating Jonathan Zeizel. During the second Canadian gig of the tour, in

Toronto on 20 January, Sam had hinted to the audience he was single again during his 'Good Thing' introduction. As previously stated, that particular song was written at the point when he had decided to take control of his previous, infamously unrequited love affair. It celebrated the moment of empowerment when someone in a doomed relationship chooses to say 'enough is enough', to not answer the call from the person who is the cause of their pain or deletes their numbers from their phone. Sam told the crowd, 'This song is very special to me today, as I've actually had to do a very similar thing with someone I've been seeing.'

After the Toronto concert, Sam thanked everyone who had been at the gig via Instagram, saying, 'Sometimes you just need to lay in bed with a glass of red wine and a football T shirt and listen to Joni Mitchell. It's been a sad day. Beautiful show, but sad day x.' He remained optimistic he'd eventually find 'Mr Right', but in the meantime, typically, he was using his own music as a source of comfort. 'Hopefully I will find someone soon and when I do I think it will be a bit more difficult to sing [my] songs because I will want to sing happy songs. Right now when I'm on stage I feel like it is good for me, it is like therapy every night... The music comforts me.'

Sam would later officially confirm the split with Zeizel in an interview with the *London Evening Standard*, when he stated, 'We just weren't very compatible. Nothing dramatic happened. I made a mistake by posting pictures of us on Instagram and making it seem more serious than it was.' Looking back on their time together, Sam would downplay the seriousness of the relationship, telling *Rolling Stone*, 'I've allowed someone to stay in my bed more than, like, three times, which is the first time that's happened in a long time,' but it's clear the whole experience had taught him a valuable lesson. He was finding out the hard way just how difficult it was to keep any relationship afloat, especially one being played out in public and across social media. 'I've learned I need to hold off before I start getting the public involved,' he told *The Sun*. 'I would say it was a relationship, but I still feel like I haven't had a proper boyfriend yet.' But as always with Sam, he remained determined his philosophy of 'living life to the full' and then writing about it would prevail and it's safe to assume there just might be a song or two dealing with this particular chapter in his life taking shape for album number two.

As for the rest of 2015, Sam's romantic life aside, things had gotten off to a pretty good start. Outside his professional triumphs, winning big at the Grammys and being told *In the Lonely Hour* had sold more than 1 million copies in both the UK and the US, making him the only artist to do so in 2014, Sam's positivity and personal well-being seemed to be at an all-time high. During his preparations for the Grammys, he stated he wanted to lose a little weight. On returning from his Australian holiday, he was confronted with shirtless tabloid pictures of himself on the beach and it reignited some of his old body-consciousness issues. 'That f*cking shot, I dreaded it,' he exclaimed to *Rolling Stone*. 'I just want to lose weight for the Grammys, if I'm honest.' But he was also reacting to cruel jibes, made across social media and from the likes of US comedian and controversial radio host Howard Stern about his weight. On his *Sirius XM* radio show, Stern said

Sam was 'an ugly motherf*cker' before calling him 'fat' and 'effeminate'. While Stern would later insist his comments were taken out of context and 'sensationalized', stating he was in fact praising him for being just a normal guy and 'beating the odds', Sam was understandably upset. At the time he tweeted, 'I can't believe what I just read... Ignore.'

But in reality, it must have hit a nerve and he couldn't just brush it off. Sam's relationship with food and his diet was a long and undoubtedly complicated one. He told *US* magazine, 'From a young age, food has controlled me basically., When I was at school and wasn't having a great time or when music wasn't going very well, I would eat. When I felt lonely, I would eat.'

He had obviously started to question some of the more negative aspects of his life and had decided to try and bring positive change where he could. 'I am gay and I'm proud to be gay so there's no issue there,' he said. 'If someone calls you fat, it's like, that's something I want to change. That affects me more.' But he was in a great place emotionally, happier than he'd been in years, and now seemed like the best time to try and break the negative cycle he'd put his body (and voice) through over the years. Previously he had tried and failed before, using 'fad' diets and programmes that promised an easy fix, so this time he began searching for something a little more radical: Sam wanted a lifestyle change. Now, he was looking for something to alter his whole attitude towards eating and food. If it helped him lose some weight, that was great, but more importantly he wanted to improve his overall health, as well as find a diet to help him take better care of his voice.

Step forward Amelia Freer, a London-based nutritionist with over a decade's experience, who after releasing a series of four, seasonally themed eBooks had just published her first full-length title, *Eat. Nourish. Glow*. Freer had given up working as a full-time personal assistant to Prince Charles, heading back to college at twenty-eight years old and, after four years of study, had secured a qualification from the Institute for Optimum Nutrition. Over the next decade, she became the nutrition therapist to the stars, offering a complete course of consultations on general health, as well as food and weight issues. After it was discovered that she was behind the recent (and much publicised) transformations enjoyed by the likes of Boy George and James Corden, Freer was approached by publishers keen to turn her ideas into a best-selling book.

Freer's overall approach is based on the paleolithic diet, a system which aims to replace harmful elements of our modern diet with the type of foodstuffs more readily available to our ancient ancestors, prior to the agricultural boom and the domestication of animals for food. Rejecting modern-day processed foods, as well as most forms of grain, refined sugar and dairy, this approach to daily nutrition is said to be more in tune with the body's natural metabolism and cuts down on present-day health problems such as diabetes, heart disease and obesity. At its core, Freer's regime introduces a series of lifestyle principles which aim to improve basic, everyday diet and alter general attitudes towards food in a way which is easy to follow and therefore less likely to fail. It promotes an understanding of what nutrition does for the body, addresses bad habits that may have built up over decades and replaces the harmful elements of our diet with healthier alternatives. Freer advocates that we should get back into the kitchen, cooking for ourselves and taking more control over the food in our diet. She told *Inquisitr*, 'It's not about being perfect, it's not about focusing on your weight, it's about cooking your food from scratch. Start with one meal a day and build up. That, for me, is the foundation of good health.'

For Sam, it was a complete revelation and, as someone who was in the public eye and very active on social media, his transformation was instantly apparent. Only three weeks after meeting Freer, he took to Instagram to sing her praises. He stated, '[Amelia Freer] has completely changed my life. [She] has helped me lose over a stone in two weeks and has completely transformed my relationship with food.' Stressing it was more than just another 'fad' diet, he went on to say, 'It's not even about weight loss, it's about feeling happy in yourself,' before addressing Freer directly, saying, 'Thank you for making me feel so happy, inside and out.'

Freer responded by telling *Inquisitr*, 'It's very nice for me to see the results that I do get with my clients. By someone like Sam talking about how he's changed his diet in a healthy way without a deprivational, horrible diet, it's opened it up to thousands of people who are now following in his footsteps.' She concluded, 'Sam has a lot of young fans, and how cool that these young kids are starting to take care of what they are eating. To me, that's beyond awesome and a dream come true.' It was certainly 'a dream come true' for her publisher because, as Sam continued to post pictures on Instagram of the healthier meals he was now enjoying and as his weight continued to plummet, Freer's book started to climb the bestsellers' lists.

While some speculated Sam's weight loss was too fast and too severe, others were quick to defend his new, healthier lifestyle. Speaking on *ABC News*, Dr Jennifer Ashton confirmed, 'Fourteen pounds in two weeks is not alarming unless a person losing that weight has any pre-existing medical problems. When you talk about eating properly, people who do have weight to lose will see dramatic results.' As Freer pointed out to *Hello! Magazine*, diet alone wasn't the answer and exercise and self-discipline also played a part. She insisted there was 'no magic potion, no fairy dust, no one to push you, no one to do it for you'. It became very clear, as time went on and his physical transformation continued, that Sam hadn't fallen victim to something 'faddy' or dangerous. He had in fact fully embraced Freer's regime, made a dramatic change to his whole lifestyle and the endless pictures of him sweating it out at the gym on Instagram were proof indeed he was taking it all very seriously. Unfortunately for Sam, this period of positive change and inner contentment was relatively short-lived as he was about to experience a serious health crisis of a completely different type, and in the process he would face his worst nightmare: losing his voice.

Sam's problems with his voice had started in the middle of the previous year. As early as June 2014, he faced dealing with the consequences of constantly straining his voice and pushing his vocal cords to their limits. On returning from gigs in the US, he had cancelled his appearance at Capital FM's Summertime Ball, releasing a statement via social media which stated, 'I am so so sad to say I won't be performing today. I've just got off the plane and my voice has completely gone. I really have to avoid any long-term damage to my voice,' before adding, 'This is the first show I've ever had to cancel and I am praying that it is the last.'

Sadly, it was not. Almost inevitably, considering his busy schedule and extensive performance diary, Sam would experience further problems throughout the year. In September, a show in Toronto, Canada, was pulled at short notice after he announced via Instagram, 'I am so unbelievably sorry but I'm going to have to cancel tonight's show. I woke up yesterday morning with tonsillitis and I didn't speak all day and all night in hopes it would clear and I'd be able to perform for you all tonight. It's worse and I can't speak.' He ended the message by saying, 'I'm so upset and will reschedule the show as soon as possible. I'm sorry.'

A couple of months later, Sam was forced to cancel another show, this time in Houston, Texas, and his voice problems continued to haunt him into the New Year – subsequent gigs in Seattle, in February, and the following month in Milan, Italy, were also postponed indefinitely. While health problems, and therefore cancellations of this type, are almost inevitable with a touring schedule like Sam's, by the time he started the Australian and New Zealand leg of the tour in April, his voice was becoming increasingly unpredictable and things would only get worse.

The dates kicked off with two nights in Auckland, New Zealand, on 22 and 23 April. And while Sam was having a degree of difficulty maintaining the power and full range of his voice, he carried on and gave the best performances he could. But by the time he reached Sydney, Australia, less than a week later, things were getting serious. Sam played the first of a two-night stay at the city's Hordern Pavilion, but was forced to cancel the second. He told fans, via Instagram, 'I am deeply, deeply saddened to tell my Australian fans I have to cancel my Australian tour,' before explaining, 'I have been vocally exhausted for a while now, however last night in Sydney I had a small haemorrhage on my vocal cords. The doctors have told me I need to fully rest until my vocal cords have healed, otherwise this could become a huge long-term issue. I am so sorry to all who have bought tickets, I truly am. This kills me.'

In some respects it was a fairly common occurrence, with countless numbers of well-known singers having gone through the same thing as Sam over the years. Dr Michael Pittman, a spokesman for The New York Eye and Ear Infirmary, stated to *CBS News*, 'It can happen to anyone who uses their voice a lot. Teachers have the highest prevalence of voice disorders.' Commonplace or not, it's safe to assume this was a particularly unsettling time for Sam and it's hard to imagine anything more frightening for a singer than experiencing damaged or bleeding vocal cords. The first course of action in these circumstances is usually to give the vocal cords a complete rest, which obviously involves no singing, and, as in Sam's case, no talking for several days. Sometimes the voice really just needs time to recover and, as another leading ear, nose and throat doctor, Jordan S. Josephson, confirmed to *CBS News*, 'Some patients just need voice therapy and they get better.' Josephson elaborated by stating even if the patient did require surgery, it was not necessarily a complicated procedure – 'Most patients come in the morning and go home the same day.'

For Sam, it was a waiting game to find out if his vocal cords would heal by themselves or whether he would need further medical attention. So instead of completing his Australian tour dates and appearing at the TV Week Logie Awards – the Australian equivalent of the UK's BAFTAs or US Emmys – Sam spent the next few days relaxing in the Australian countryside. After a few days, he contacted his fans via Instagram to say, 'I'm ok. I am insanely relaxed and am somewhere in the middle of Australia with no phone, no laptop and I haven't spoken a word in three days.' He continued, 'Trying my absolute best to be back on my feet and singing for next week. So amazing to have this time off, but it does make me realise how much I love what I do, and how much I miss you all when I'm not on stage,' before signing off with, 'I'm gonna go back to my black and white movies and pretend I'm Judy Garland for a few more days xx.'

But in the end, it was nothing but bad news for Sam (and his fans), as it quickly became apparent his vocal cords were not healing on their own and the remainder of his short-term touring schedule and appearances were cancelled. Sam announced via Facebook, 'I am very upset to announce I have been battling to get my vocal cords better the last 10 days. But unfortunately they haven't recovered and I am going to need surgery. I'm so gutted to be missing all the shows and events I was meant to be playing at.'

Sam had flown to the US to see a specialist surgeon and together they came to the decision that an operation would be needed to correct the issues he was having with his vocal cords. He broke the news to fans via his Instagram page: 'Bad news. I have my operation booked for next week, so getting really nervous. But doing this in eight weeks' time I'm gonna be able to sing like never before so it's worth it. Dreading the next month thou, I can't speak for three weeks after the op.'

Categorised simply as 'corrective voice surgery', he was due to undergo a procedure to stop the bleeding caused by unstable blood vessels in his vocal cords. His treatment involved laser surgery that seals the bleeding blood vessels. If left untreated, or in more serious cases, the vocal cords can become even more damaged, rupturing and often leading to lesions (also known as 'nodules' and 'polyps'), which can make it difficult for a patient to speak and virtually impossible to sing. In these more extreme cases, it would necessitate slightly more invasive microscopic surgery to remove them.

On 13 May, the night before his operation, Sam tweeted his fans, saying, 'Can't sleep. Op tomorrow. Looking through all your beautiful messages. Makes me emotional to know I have so many people wishing me well.' Thankfully, he wasn't just relying on his fans for support, as his mum, Kate, flew out to the States to be with him while he was hospitalised. Sam's surgery took place at the Massachusetts General Hospital in Boston and was performed by Dr Steven Zeitels, a leading expert in his field. He is credited with inventing new techniques in the area of vocal cord surgery and, as a result of his work, operations were less invasive, more accurate and, in turn, recovery times had been significantly reduced in recent years. Previously, Zeitel's experience had seen him perform similar operations on several other famous clients, including Adele, Lionel Richie and Aerosmith's Steven Tyler.

As expected, Sam's operation was a relatively simple one and he was discharged from hospital the next day. Keeping his fans up to date with everything that was going on, he tweeted, 'Just touched down in London Town x good to be home. Although I'm already get pissed off with not speaking.' In an official announcement released by Sam's team on 19 May, his twenty-third birthday, it was reported that the operation was a complete success and it was now just a matter of letting his voice recover.

Sam was obviously holding court at home and, aside from his alcohol-fuelled (but obviously silent) birthday party, he was receiving visits from many of his closest friends and much of 'Team Sam Smith'. His songwriting partner Jimmy Napes told BBC Radio 1's *Newsbeat*, 'He's doing well, he's resting up,' before revealing exactly how Sam was managing to communicate with everyone. Napes said, 'He's got an app that speaks for him and it's like Stephen Hawking, where you type something in, except it's in a girl's voice – which is hilarious.' While this throws up all kinds of possibilities for Sam's next album, bringing to mind some of Prince's more extreme vocal experiments and his female 'alter-ego', Camille, who sang on 1987's 'If I Was Your Girlfriend', Napes was quick to dismiss any possibilities of this voice turning up on record, saying, 'It might be a little outtake on the new album.'

Sam was expected to fully rest his voice for the next couple of months. There would obviously be a short period of therapy and vocal exercises to get everything back to normal, with him due to make his next scheduled appearance at an outdoor concert in Suffolk's Thetford Forest on 3 July. If everything went to plan, he would be back on the road for much of the summer, with several European festival dates and a full US arena tour to complete before the end of August.

Sam had been relatively lucky. He appeared to have caught the problem in its earliest stages and his surgery was carried out swiftly, and apparently successfully. If he was, yet again, looking to Adele for inspiration and as a role model, he must have taken some comfort from the fact that she also underwent similar surgery in 2011, and, let's just say, that didn't work out too badly for her during the couple of years which followed.

CHAPTER FIFTEEN

NO MORE
LONELY NIGHTS

'The minute I started to tell a story, everything clicked into place. I became an artist because I had something to say.'
Sam Smith on the difference between being a pop star
and an artist – *Teen Vogue*, November 2014

A fter three weeks of torturous silence, and a few days after his voice doctors gave him the all-clear and he was allowed to speak again, Sam took to social media platforms to thank the man who had performed his life- (or rather voice-) saving operation. Alongside a picture of himself with the respected US surgeon, Sam said, 'Completely overwhelmed. Thank you so much Doctor Zeitels for everything. You have truly saved me this past few months,' before adding, 'Such an amazing man.'

While it's hardly surprising he would take the opportunity to show just how grateful he was for his doctor's skills and to thank the man who operated on him, it seems Sam's period of quiet contemplation had caused a slightly more unexpected epiphany. He went on to exclaim, 'You truly, truly don't know what you got until you lose it. I have fallen in love with music all over again over this past month, and more than ever I feel so blessed to be able to sing and do what I love every day.' All of which bodes well for the next, all-important chapter in his career.

Sam was now at an important crossroads in his life. Finally, he had managed to set down some roots of his own, moving into a newly acquired London home during his recovery period. He had experienced a couple of fairly 'nomadic' years, what with world tours and being forced to move flats due to a couple of burglaries in the spring and summer of 2014. Finding 'his own place', at this particular moment, seemed symbolic. An air of calm appears to have settled on his entire life and it is in this relative peace that he must be thinking about 'Phase 2'.

While they don't call it 'Difficult Second Album Syndrome' for nothing, embarking on the process of creating the follow-up to your debut record can be a daunting, but undoubtedly exciting challenge. A recognised phenomenon in education circles, where it's often referred to as 'sophomore slump', in the music industry it can completely derail careers – just ask Terence Trent D'Arby, The Stone Roses and Duffy. But for every *Neither Fish Nor Flesh* and *The Second Coming*, there's the second album which can be ranked among the most undisputed of classics, such as Radiohead's *The Bends*, Carole King's *Tapestry*, *Nevermind* by Nirvana, or, perhaps more relevant to Sam, *21* by Adele. Adele's habit of naming her albums after the age she was when she recorded them – *19* and then *21* – indicate a respectable two-year gap between releases – although if the rumours are true and there's no new record on the horizon, we could be waiting a long time for album No.3, provisionally titled *41*. If Sam's career is to follow that of Adele's as closely as most media outlets and music journalists seem to want it to, his next album should appear sometime in 2016. In the meantime we just might be able to look forward to a seasonal re-pack of *In the Lonely Hour* for Christmas 2015, and no one seems to doubt his suitability to supply the new James Bond movie, *Spectre*, with a typically epic and timeless theme song. But in terms of the contents of his actual second album, Sam has already hinted at the direction he would prefer to take his songs and how different writing and recording locations might become as important an inspiration as London was for *In the Lonely Hour*.

Putting the last couple of years into perspective and reflecting on who he was when he wrote the songs for *In the Lonely Hour*, Sam told *Fader*, 'At twenty-two, you're still very much figuring out your identity. I don't know [who I am] and I'm really not trying to pretend like I know.' But with that chapter of his life now more or less over, he was inevitably taking stock of everything he'd learned in the process and thinking about what his next move should be. 'I know I want to be a singer, and it makes me feel good,' he stated, 'Even going back to the writing thing – sometimes I go into the session and want to be like Beyoncé, so I try to do Beyoncé songs. But the only songs that work are the ones where I'm being myself.'

Sam's idea of 'being himself' was very much to the fore whenever the subject of album No.2 came up and it would seem his change of circumstances was preying heavily on his mind. 'After *In the Lonely Hour*, I was thinking, "How do I become relatable when I'm not relatable?",' he explained to *Rolling Stone*. '[Most] people don't go to [fancy] restaurants, can't treat their families and take their sisters out. People don't have that. And how could I write an album that people can relate to when people can't relate to [me]?' Already feeling the pressure to find new experiences and emotions to write about, he stated, '[I had] that pressure of, "OK, shit, now I need to fall in love. Something like that needs to happen for me to become relatable again."' I could lose everything on my second album, because I'm no longer relatable.'

It seems Sam's overriding desire to represent the things he experienced in his life – good and bad – in the songs he wrote and recorded was as strong as ever and he has already vowed to keep pushing that particular envelope. 'I'm getting really excited about my new record,' he told *Mclean's* at the start of 2015. 'With [*In the Lonely Hour*] I only dealt with loneliness but the next album, the [themes] will be broader.' He expanded on his need to strip away the layers and reveal more of his true self in an interview with *Rolling Stone*, where he promised his next record would challenge people's preconceptions and 'change what a pop star is'. Elaborating further, he said, 'I'm very passionate about being relatable. On my second record, instead of looking like I have more money, more airbrushing, I want to actually be more raw and honest on my second album than my first. I want to be a pop star that isn't really skinny, a pop star who doesn't have a perfectly even face… I think that's deep down what I really want to do in music. I want to change that whole idea of, "When I'm older, I want to be perfect". I want to change people's idea of what perfection is.'

In the Lonely Hour had given Sam opportunities he could only have dreamed about previously, and he'd added some impressive names to his phonebook, but all the pleasant surprises also brought a similarly unexpected level of pressure. He had often fantasised about success and its accompanying lifestyle, but his feelings towards some elements had shocked him. Sam told *Fader*, 'Two years ago, I thought I was going to be a guy who was going to love parties and love mixing with stars, and be that kind of guy who soaks up the whole fame side of it. But the more I get into this, it's the only part that makes me uncomfortable.' Perhaps he was learning the true value of having 'the right team' around him, and in the end, it would undoubtedly be those people who had guided him to this point who would help steer him through whatever came next. The fear of failure, of losing everything he'd worked for so far, which Sam has carried with him most of his life, might feel particularly crippling at this very moment. While he often links these concerns to his mother's professional misfortunes, she had also taught him the value of resilience, determination and never losing sight of what drives you.

Discussing the idea of trying to follow up his debut and dealing with a possible backlash, Sam told the *Guardian*, 'Every day it gets a little bit more insane. I get good news every day. I'm so scared for when that's going to stop, if it's going to stop. It's reminding me of that time when my mum had so much money and then all the people she thought were her closest friends disappeared.' For him, he reasoned, it might be just as brutal, as he speculated to the *Telegraph*: 'One day I might bring out a really shit album. It will be interesting to see who's still your friend then.'

As fleeting as fame can be, Sam already seemed to have his head screwed on and was well aware that there was a difference between making a huge initial impact on the music scene and making it last. The manifesto he'd put in place for *In the Lonely Hour* was more relevant now than it was at the very start of that project – Sam wanted the music he made to be timeless and to have real substance. He told *Fader*, 'I want to make the music that's not there anymore. I'm passionate about the singing voice. I watch artists around me that have 200 fans waiting outside of hotels and venues for them and they can't sing. All I ask for is a balance between people who can make thousands of girls scream, and people who can deliver and make music that can stand the test of time.'

Sam has stated that *In the Lonely Hour* was an album wholly about him and his voice – personal in terms of subject matter and in that there were no vocal collaborations featured on the record. He told *Pigeons and Planes*, 'I really just wanted this first album to be all about me. This album almost feels like they've said, "Naughty Boy and Disclosure have gone. There you go, it's your time." I like that it's all about me.'

But over the last year or so, he has formed some close friendships with some very important artists and musicians. With Disclosure's second album on the horizon, it's fairly likely there will be another guest vocalist spot for Sam on a track or two and beyond that, he has numerous duet partners ready and willing to join him in the studio. Whatever his intentions for this particular album, in recent times he has undoubtedly been creating a mental wish-list of future singing partners. Close to home, surely top of his list has to be Jessie Ware, his old PMR buddy. He told *P&P*, 'I really wanna do a duet with her, I really do. She's incredible and also my friend and is actually the loveliest girl I've ever met in this industry.' Slightly more left-field is Sam's admiration for Antony Hegarty (of Antony and the Johnsons fame). Sam confessed to *Mclean's*, 'I fancy his voice so much. He makes music that makes you want to bawl and provokes such huge emotions inside. I'd love to meet him; doing a duet with him is something I'd one million per cent love to do.'

But Sam's impact overseas has left his contacts book bursting at the seams with international stars. Already he has appeared on stage with Taylor Swift, although it's hard to imagine the song which would suit them both if they ever got into a studio together, and his association with the legendary Mary J. Blige has already borne fruit – a duet version of 'Stay With Me' for Sam and material for Blige's *London Sessions* album. Despite telling *Mclean's*, 'I don't think I'll have anyone on my next record. I want to save duets and collaborations for outside of the album,' it's hard to imagine Sam turning down a call from his ultimate duet partner – Beyoncé. While she has reportedly said his voice was 'like butter' and there's no shortage of mutual respect, he has yet to spend any time with his idol. Sam told GQ he was worried meeting her might be a mistake, stating, 'If you meet everyone you're inspired by you'll have no one to look up to.' But it seems unlikely he'd be content to stick with the 'Beyoncé's bath water' mug he was gifted by a fan, should the chance arise.

In terms of co-writers for his next project, aside from expressing his desire to re-team with the likes of Ben Ash

(Two Inch Punch), Fraser T. Smith and, of course, Jimmy Napes, Sam has stated he is much more open to new blood. He told *Mclean's*, 'I'd love to work with Gaga, Chaka Khan and Ryan Tedder.' Stylistically, it's easy to see he wants to take his music into previously uncharted territory. Conscious of the overall influence London had on his first record – through the loneliness he imagines permeates the whole city and his own associations and personal history with the place – it's become increasingly clear Sam wants his second record to reflect something else, or rather somewhere else.

'I definitely want to move to New York City for my second album,' he told *Pigeons and Planes*, 'If I get the opportunity to do it, I wanna be somewhere else. I think it's important to be inspired by different places when you write music.'

With over 4 million album sales under his belt it would seem likely, for the foreseeable future at least, Sam will be able to go wherever he wants, for as long as he wants and no one is going to tell him otherwise. In terms of new musical influences, he has recently been branching out from his beloved big-voiced divas. Expressing his ladmiration for D'Angelo, the US R&B-soul singer whose *Black Messiah* album had been on constant repeat on his stereo, Sam also told *Pigeons and Planes*, 'I'm getting into my soul music a lot more now. I'm delving a lot into Prince and Luther Vandross.'

Whatever new directions Sam intends to explore within his music, and whatever journey he wants his listeners to experience next, he isn't leaving anything to chance. As he told *Digital Spy* only a few months after the release of his first album, 'I'm a complete control freak so I've already decided on the artwork and title of the album.' While conceding this would more than likely change in time, he was adamant he needed to stay one step ahead of the curve. 'I think I will always be so scared of not doing this as a career,' he admitted. 'So the thought of just sitting back and enjoying the ride, and then late next year someone going, "Right, now we need to do [a] second album", and me not knowing what the f*ck to do… I couldn't do that.'

Apparently with this in mind, Sam has already revealed the title of one song (and its subject matter) likely to appear on his sophomore effort. After playing an early version of the song 'Scars' to a *Rolling Stone* journalist, he asked, 'Do you like it? It's just an insight to how personal I'm going to go with the second record.' A gut-wrenching ballad, which acts as a letter to his parents about their divorce, 'Scars' seems to have already made its mark within various strands of the Smith family. Sam explained, 'It's very deep. I've only played it for my family. They cried every single time I played it,' before concluding, 'Every kid who has come from a divorced family is going to listen to that.'

As he enters the next phase of his life, Sam seems as determined as ever to heed the words of wisdom given to him by his idol, Lady Gaga, shortly after he'd arrived in the US. He told *Vibe*, 'Lady Gaga was on the *Ryan Seacrest Show* and she said, "I just hope that Sam stays himself and carries on being himself."' Stating it was the best advice he'd been given by anyone in 'The Business' so far, he continued, 'She's someone I've looked up to my whole life and for her to say that about me was such an incredible moment. That's all I need to do. Stop worrying and stop trying to look like a supermodel or try and sound like a certain type of artist and just be myself and enjoy it.'

With this in mind, it seems Sam has vowed to continue living life to the full, grabbing each new experience with both hands and squeezing every last drop of inspiration he can from it – however personal or painful that may be. He explained to *Fader*, 'I feel like I've got quite an old head on my shoulders. I want to let go and have fun a bit more, but I want to be wise. I want to see the world. I want to be rich in all the foods I've tasted and all the places I've been and all the people I've kissed. I want to be rich in every single way.'

If he can deliver on this promise, his time in the 'lonely hour' might be well and truly over and finally he can look ahead, with hopeful optimism, to whatever comes next. While that might not seem like the perfect recipe for more lovelorn songs about rejection and loneliness, whatever happens in Sam Smith's next chapter will undoubtedly be just as inspiring. Whether he finds the man of his dreams or more disappointments and heartbreak, it's safe to imagine there will be at least a handful of songs written in celebration or as therapy, and whatever the circumstances, we'll be happy to sing along.

And if he does find himself back 'in the lonely hour', at least this time he has an army of 'little sailors' to comfort him – and if that's not enough, there's always Taylor, Katy, Gaga and Rihanna on his speed dial!